rEvolution

Turn CRISIS Into CLARITY and IGNITE
GROWTH

TIM LEMAN with Larry G. Linne

Foreword by **Joe Calloway** Author of
Be the Best at What Matters Most

authorHOUSE®

AuthorHouse™
1663 Liberty Drive
Bloomington, IN 47403
www.authorhouse.com
Phone: 1 (800) 839-8640

Published by AuthorHouse   03/04/2015

ISBN: 978-1-4969-6691-9 (sc)
ISBN: 978-1-4969-6693-3 (hc)
ISBN: 978-1-4969-6692-6 (e)

Library of Congress Control Number: 2015901520

Printed in the United States of America by BookMasters, Inc
Ashland OH
July 2015

Contents

Foreword – Joe Calloway
Author of *Be The Best At What Matters Most*

When I read a great book, a book that truly has something of real value to say, I find myself making a mental list of the people that I want to give it to.

The list of people to whom I will send a copy of Tim Leman's new book, *rEvolution - Turn Crisis Into Clarity And Ignite Growth*, grew with every chapter that I read. First and foremost are my clients, who depend on me to give them sound advice on how effective leadership can improve performance and grow a business. I can think of nothing more beneficial to my clients than to have them read this book.

Tim doesn't give us a written lecture about the theoretical or academic keys to effective leadership. Instead, Tim tells us a story. It's a story that thousands of business leaders, owners, and managers will relate to, not just in their minds, but in their gut. As you read this book, you will almost certainly be thinking "I have been there," or "I am there right now."

Leadership isn't for wimps, and rEvolution doesn't sugarcoat the extremely difficult, stressful, and sometimes seemingly overwhelming challenges that leaders face. Tim's own story begins with a simple, yet powerful letter that he wrote to his business partners. It was an act that took great courage, and it began a journey over the next few years that included victories, small and large, and a fair share of self-doubt and defeats.

It's the real world honesty of Tim's story that I believe makes it so valuable. Every leader will see example after example that mirrors their own journey, and Tim's insights are reassuring and revelatory.

A leader must make tough choices, and live with the consequences. Some of the principals that I learned or had vividly reinforced in rEvolution include:

- Change is constant. Just when you think you understand the situation, the situation has changed. The effective leader must always adjust.

- As a leader changes, he/she must also provide a foundation of stability to the organization. That foundation is culture.

- You must be open to other perspectives, other ideas, constructive push-back, and criticism that challenge your sense of self.

- Maybe above all, a leader must bring clarity. Clarity about who we are, and about what matters most to you, and to your clients. A lack of clarity slows you down, scatters your efforts, and makes for bad decisions.

- Once you get that clarity on who you are and what matters most, a leader must communicate effectively and continuously. Culture only takes hold through reinforcement, and it's the leader's job to over-communicate.

Rather than give you any further outline of the content in this remarkable book, let me share what that content meant to me personally.

The greatest, most valuable lesson that Tim teaches me in rEvolution is the lesson of courage. Any leader that is going to take an organization forward…that is going to grow the business and keep it relevant in a constantly changing marketplace…is going to have to make courageous decisions. Perhaps an even more valuable lesson is that some of those decisions are most assuredly going to be wrong.

How you personally deal with the setbacks and defeats that are an inherent part of the journey in business leadership is vitally important. Most important is to learn from the mistakes and use that new insight and information to continue to move forward. True leaders aren't infallible. Indeed, truly great leaders are among the most human of us all.

One of the other impactful lessons in rEvolution for me is how a great leader is not only able to learn and grow from very tough feedback, but invites and embraces it. It's hard to hear others criticize your leadership. It's personal. It just plain hurts. But to rise above that pain and use constructive criticism to grow and become better, stronger, and more effective - this is a hallmark of a truly great leader.

My job for over thirty years has been to advise and teach business leaders, owners, managers, and entrepreneurs how to make a great company even better. For me to remain relevant to my clients, I have to constantly grow and learn. I have to know what works in business, and more specifically, what works in leadership. I am a voracious reader, and I read dozens of business books each year.

Tim Leman's rEvolution is a business leadership book that receives my highest recommendation.

I wish you good reading. You are about to become a better leader.

Introduction – Larry G. Linne

Leadership is complex and dynamic. It is ever-changing because it is about people, and people change, cultures change, the motivators to be followed change. Evolution demands that leaders must adjust to inspire others to follow.

As an advisor to some of the top business leaders in North America I have observed the impact of economics, culture, politics and many other factors influencing how leaders lead. Some leaders have failed. They have rigidly held onto behaviors that were strongholds of leadership for multiple generations. Now, those behaviors have turned their leadership to loneliness. They are no longer followed.

It has also been a blessing to watch and guide some amazing leaders to evolve into a new generation of leaders. These leaders understand human behavior and recognize what it takes to inspire others to follow. They recognize the power of intrinsic motivation, connecting to the heart of people, and serving people in ways that make others hungry to follow.

We are in a unique time in business in which we have transitioned from evolution to revolution in buying behaviors, employee expectations, employee behaviors, information availability, and generational influence. I have been tracking emerging challenges to leadership over the past few years. It's difficult to keep up with ever-changing elements to become or remain a powerful leader. However, these emerging leadership challenges must be addressed. I continue to be diligent in tracking and testing strategies for success and advise my clients to do the same.

Many leaders of the past were able to have a single leadership style and practice through an entire career. They were able to lead a certain type of employee that was established, stable, and consistent.

Now we have dynamics within the workforce that challenge even the most skilled leader. The people we are leading are more diverse and have different expectations of why they work and what they want to accomplish. This diversity is going to bring new pressure on leaders to change.

The emerging issues are going to challenge leaders in ways they have not been challenged in the past. Leaders that plan to ride it out without evolving will find themselves sitting alone and failing. Leaders that embrace change and evolve with new needs and expectations will have great success and reward.

One of the executives I have worked with over the past five years is Tim Leman. He has an exciting story and I've been encouraging him to share it. His authentic and transparent telling of his struggles and growth in leadership will serve as inspiration to other leaders and organizations.

He's made adjustments, pushing through uncomfortable exercises required to lead. He has committed to become a leader of the future. I have no doubt that Tim will have a legacy in his career that is centered around his leadership.

Tim was also the right leader at the right time at his organization. By most accounts, Gibson Insurance Agency, Inc., had very successfully been in business since 1933 in the northern Indiana marketplace. They didn't need Tim Leman as their leader to stay in business. However it's likely their independence – something they and other leading insurance brokers hold sacred – was at risk.

Tim's influence and personal growth over the past few years has been inspiring to watch. He has led and executed significant change in the organization with impressive positive financial results mirroring those changes.

As any great leader would communicate, Tim has not done it alone. His partners, leadership teams, board of directors, and staff have all played a huge part in his ability to lead. I've had the pleasure of meeting and working with many of them. They are an inspired and driven group of people! Tim knows he couldn't have accomplished any goal in the company without the collaboration and commitment of his team.

Most firms will never create a story worthy to be told or read in a book. The Gibson story is one that falls in the "must read" category. It's one of leadership evolution (and at times revolution), understanding people, taking chances, innovation, managing diversity, and much more. The reader will gain insight into high impact leadership techniques and strategies.

This book will spark awareness in new areas of leadership that are critical to current business environments. Tim's historical account of the company will certainly fill the reader with practical insights to leading an effective organization. But it's his current and future thinking that will set the reader on the path for a great future. The understanding of Tim's personal growth, leadership evolution, and journey from chaos and confusion to clarity will inspire immediate action.

Leadership is changing. The diversity of the people we lead will single-handedly require change. Add technology, generational polarization, economic uncertainty, innovation in HR, and numerous other influencers, and you will clearly see how leadership will look different in the future.

Tim's journey shows how introspection, courage, resiliency, and continuous development on his leadership capabilities changed an organization and made it one of the top insurance agencies in North America. I was blessed to be part of his story and teach, inspire, and collaborate with him at the perfect time in his leadership life.

I hope you enjoy the story and the experience as much as those who lived it.

Chapter 1 – A Very Good Company

With one more scan of an email I had entitled "An Open Letter to My Fellow Partners", I took a deep breath, paused for a second and hit the send button. There would be no turning back now. Courtesy of their newest partner, all of my fellow owners were about to receive a very honest but stinging critique on how we were doing as a company. I shut my home computer down, grabbed my car keys and drove to the airport with my wife, Kimra. It was May 15, 2007. We were off to New York City to celebrate our 10th wedding anniversary. Things were about to get very interesting at Gibson.

Before I tell you more about "The Letter", and my evolution as a leader, I have to put some context around it. While my story spans a multi-year period, it's important for you understand what an amazing organization Gibson had been for nearly three quarters of a century.

Gibson Insurance Agency, Inc. was founded in 1933 in the small northern Indiana town of Plymouth by Dan Gibson. The depression was still underway. There was little local industry and the economy was primarily based on agriculture and local retail firms.

Dan's original focus was life insurance. He had a strong will to succeed and soon won the confidence of the many families and businesses he began to serve. In his second year in business he sold 30 new policies in one month to lead all the agents in Northwestern Mutual's northern Indiana territory.

He saw an opportunity to expand his business and started to sell auto, fire, and theft coverage to his growing client base. Dan and company fought through the challenging times of the 1930s and established the agency's reputation for hard work and impeccable ethics.

When World War II broke out in 1942, Dan joined the US Navy. He left for the Pacific theater as an aircraft operations control officer on the USS Attu, an escort aircraft carrier. He returned to the agency in 1945.

The 1950s saw Dan and other community leaders in Plymouth start to focus on ways to entice manufacturing firms to locate in the area. This led to the formation of the Plymouth Industrial Development Corporation (PIDCO). Funds were raised and land was purchased to form the first industrial park.

Dan stayed very active in local and state insurance associations during the 1960s. These were early forerunners for Gibson to the industry peer groups his son Dave would join. Dan also began Gibson's long tradition of engagement in the community. He was responsible for resurrecting the failed Community Chest and helped found the United Way of Marshall County.

Dan's son Dave took over the organization and helped modernize Gibson during the 1970s and 80s. Dave led Gibson's evolution from a "main street" insurance agency into a leading commercial insurance intermediary, or broker, in northern Indiana. Several significant milestones, such as crafting our first strategic plan and a vision of the future, occurred during this period.

The Gibsons began to transfer ownership to others in the company. They invited several non-family members to participate as stockholders. Dave knew the value in creating an ownership culture amongst his top producers.

Plans for growth were made. Continuing education – before it was required by licensing standards – and a focus on professional development would be expected of all employees. Additionally core values were put to writing and became a part of the company culture. Community support and involvement with not-for-profits was practiced faithfully in words and deeds. It was very clear to anyone that worked with Gibson that their clients, employees and community mattered a lot.

"Two things that Dave Gibson really stressed early on were continuing professional education and what we used to call computerization," commented Greg Downes, who joined the firm in 1980 and became a partner in 1982. Greg would go on to fill a number of leadership roles including President, CEO and Chairman of the Board.

He added, "It really raised the bar for who we recruited, what one had to commit to once hired and how much we were going to invest in our people and our resources. That sounds like nothing today but it was a big deal back then when no one our size was doing that kind of thing. We mandated professionalism and invested in development when few others did."

> *"We mandated professionalism and invested in development when few others did."*
> *~ Greg Downes*

There was never a question of ethics or integrity. It was well known at Gibson that whether it was in our relationships with clients or insurance companies, as well as internally with our own people, we would always do the right thing.

The introduction of non-family members as owners required a new style of leadership and collaboration. No longer could decisions realistically be made by just one person. With others owning a "piece of the rock" they expected some say in how the company operated. This shift from 100% family ownership spurred on greater engagement with key stakeholders in the company.

It also forced the ownership group to create a more formal perpetuation plan for other future partners. Those buying stock wanted a consistent way of annually valuing the company as they acquired shares from the Gibson family. They also wanted a clear picture and process for others that were offered an opportunity to buy into the company. Ultimately that next generation of buyers would purchase their shares in the same way this group bought stock from Dave Gibson. The philosophy of building a legacy and perpetuating the independent culture at Gibson had begun.

Gibson also began to focus on specialization as a business strategy. Salespeople would work on business insurance, like property and liability coverages, or on employee benefits like health insurance, but not both. Additionally many salespeople began to select industry specialties, such as manufacturing, public entities or construction, where they would hone their skills.

This also brought with it changes in the compensation structure for salespeople. Gibson established a minimum account size, something most agencies of similar size and location shied away from. These strategies and tactics were meant to drive focus on the ideal client for the salesperson. They might receive a little less compensation on each account allowing for company reinvestment in client resources and service help. This would allow the salespeople to do better and higher end work for more clients. It ultimately drove more and faster growth and higher income potential for the sales team.

At Dave's direction we joined a major national peer group, where we were one of the smallest members. At the meetings Dave regularly compared our results with successful insurance brokers from around the country. Cutting edge ideas from bigger markets were borrowed, tweaked and customized for our local client base. Key performance indicators were created to help drive a focus on the most important things.

In 1986 Gibson opened a new office in South Bend, Indiana. The focus on quality and consistency lead to significant growth in the number and size of clients.

Gibson continued to innovate as the 1990s rolled in. We hired people with safety engineering and loss prevention backgrounds. This focus on preventive risk management consulting changed our approach with clients as we shifted from just securing a good price on coverage to adding value to their organization. We began providing fee-based services to clients and also placing their insurance coverages for a fee in lieu of commissions paid by the insurance company. This was a big departure from the industry standard practice of accepting a percentage of the premiums for securing coverage.

Our foray into fee-based consulting work for clients began to shift how clients thought of us and our role. No longer were we just a "middle man" beating up insurance companies and delivering a quote for coverage. Instead, for

> *Our foray into fee-based consulting work for clients began to shift how clients thought of us and our role.*

many, their perception of Gibson shifted to that of a key trusted advisor. Yes, we would still work to secure the best value for them in the insurance marketplace, but we would also strive to control their costs in a more proactive way. If our safety engineers could provide training and workflow consulting to one of our manufacturing clients that prevented workers compensation accidents from happening, they would experience lower claims and therefore better pricing from the insurance company (let alone the cultural boost of not having as many serious accidents).

Just as powerful was the shift that began to take root internally at Gibson. Our own people saw the additional value we were providing and it felt great to be having such an impact on our clients and their businesses. This prompted ideas on how we might expand this concept even further. By the end of the decade we had a staff of 60 employees and nine partners and a growing reputation as risk management experts.

The 2000s witnessed continued success and growth. We entered into a formal business continuation plan. The agreement outlined how shares of stock could be bought and sold as well as guides for distributing profits to those owning stock. This continuation plan essentially forced an even more professional and transparent culture inside the ownership group. There were no secrets, right down to an annual disclosure of the Executive Leadership Team's compensation with the other partners.

This planned transition of ownership would help ensure the future independence of the company. This was in stark contrast to many peer companies who planned to sell or frankly didn't plan at all. Greg Downes was named President and CEO. Dave Gibson remained as Chairman but transitioned his accounts and sold his remaining equity to others in the firm. Revenues and profitability were at an all-time high.

Not long after that, in the summer of 2005, I received a call from Dave Gibson. Dave and I sat on an advisory board at Indiana State University.

I was living in Scottsdale, Arizona, and heading up the employee benefits practice in the southwestern United States for one of the national public insurance brokers.

"You need to move back home," said Dave in his typical right-to-the-point style. To which I replied with a chuckle, "Dave, I think people leave Indiana for Arizona, not the other way around."

He went on to tell me about Gibson's plans for growth. Things were good and they had turned their sights on growing the employee benefits division, something I knew a lot about. He also told me that they were thinking long term about leadership perpetuation, which he knew I had an interest in. He articulated the value everyone at Gibson placed on independence. Decisions were made locally. Resources were allocated when and where they were needed. Hiring kept up with the growth.

Still not convinced, I did tell him I was visiting family in Indiana later that month. I agreed to come see him and hung up the phone.

Until that call, the idea of moving back to Indiana and having a career at Gibson had not even entered my thoughts. Little did I know that one call would lead to a complete evolution in my leadership style and skills. What Dave didn't realize that day is that he couldn't have called me at a better time. I was miserable and planning a change. And number one on my list was leaving the culture of a large national public advisory firm.

The Phoenix office of the national company was one of the top performers in North America. It was a crown jewel within the organization.

It was my second job out of college and my first exposure to a high performing operation. There were significant expectations on salespeople. When someone left, one former boss was fond of saying, "We don't retreat. We just reload!" And we'd be on to the next one. I had little to compare it to and assumed it was the only way to achieve success. I've often referred to it as a smash mouth sales culture.

Things began to change after our global IPO sputtered. The corporate strategy to fix this was to essentially change leadership in many of the local offices and practices, coupled with an aggressive expense control initiative region-by-region. I began to see the hollowness of our model. It was a very short term play. Our limited investment dollars were spent on flashy new hires and other quarterly initiatives that Wall Street valued.

I'll never forget when the global CEO attempted to rally a large gathering of key leaders and sales talent by unequivocally stating that our focus would be on the stockholder. He went on to say that many companies mistakenly focus on their clients or their employees. If you don't take care of your owner, you won't stay in business long. What good would you be for your clients and employees then?

You can imagine the sobering looks on the faces in this key employee group as I scanned the room. Even worse, when we returned back to the branch offices, we realized word of "the stockholder is king" philosophy had already made its way back to the service teams.

While I understood the point he was trying to make, I never could reconcile my personal beliefs and values to his way of thinking. For the first time in my working career, I wasn't having any fun. I was planning my departure when I got that call from Dave.

I had been mulling over starting my own company. Due to non-compete issues with my broker role, I had even listened to a pitch from one of the local insurance carriers for their market president role. One thing I had never considered was joining a small insurance agency. And with apologies to John Mellencamp, certainly not one in a small town back in Indiana!

The truth is I had spent nine years in the large national insurance consulting world. Like many career people in that space, I had developed a strong disdain for "insurance agents" even though I didn't really know what went on inside smaller insurance agencies and brokerages. I pictured plaid pants and white shoes. Perhaps even a bolo tie to top it off. I was in Arizona after all.

And I was convinced that they had no tools and resources to help their clients solve problems. I often wondered and was embarrassed by the notion that I shared the same professional license with "them".

My goal was simply to get away from the large bureaucratic control and meddling that comes with public companies and some private equity environments. I thought about starting a boutique consulting operation. I felt that would give me more direct control over my destiny and the opportunity to fully realize my potential over and above income. I still wanted to deliver serious value to my clients. And above all else it would need to be very professional.

While creating my own firm in Arizona was a strong consideration, I had not been able to accept the administrative burden and detail work that comes with starting my own business. And I couldn't get over going head-to-head with my current friends and colleagues at the national firm. Once my non-compete agreement ended, I would have to aggressively pursue former clients. That would likely cause an end to some special friendships.

Once I had opened the door to a considering a return to Indiana, I even talked seriously with some larger independent insurance brokers in Indianapolis. I worried that my ability to really have a voice in their most important decisions would still remain limited. They tried to convince me otherwise, but I couldn't see it.

I told one of these family ownership groups that one thing I knew in life was just how far I had over-married. Since that part of my life was happily settled, there would obviously be no marrying into his family. And I had not seen anyone achieve the kind of seat at the table I wanted without being a part of his family. I would only be exchanging my current corporate yolk for a new one.

The more I talked with Dave and Greg, the more the Gibson opportunity unexpectedly resonated in nearly every way. I had an opportunity to re-tool and build a thriving and lucrative employee benefits practice from the ground up. And to do it the way I knew in my gut would be powerful and sustainable for years to come. If I delivered the goods, they promised to give me an opportunity to be a relatively large investor within a year of joining. I would have a voice and real influence on the overall direction of the company.

Finally, through my in depth discussions with Dave and Greg, I realized that Gibson didn't have a longer term solution for leadership perpetuation. In my heart of hearts, that especially resonated in a big way. I had been intently studying and reflecting on the concept and practice of leadership. I had a growing fire

> *I was ready to move beyond being a successful salesperson and income generator to a role with greater impact and legacy.*

inside to be an integral part of a great organization where the mission mattered. I was ready to move beyond being a successful salesperson and income generator to a role with greater impact and legacy.

In the end, it was the opportunity with Gibson that represented the best blend of what I was looking for. It was much larger and with a longer track record than a start-up but without (I thought) all the layers of inflexibility that comes with a large company.

Gibson's commitment to remaining independent was hugely important to me as well. The brokerage segment of the insurance industry was going through a consolidation phase. The last thing I wanted to do was leave my position in Arizona only to have the firm I join sell to a national aggregator. I would be right back in the same boat. This equaled failure in my book.

I began working my network for information on Gibson and the Indiana marketplace. During my due diligence in 2005, I would confirm time and again what a highly respected and well thought of company Gibson was. Ethics and integrity? Check. Focus on helping their employees grow and develop? Check. Reputation for working hard on their clients' behalf? Check.

At the same time, I also heard things like:
- They can be a little rigid
- They're pretty formal
- They need to have a little more fun
- They're all business all the time

Lastly it would require a significant financial sacrifice to make the move. Besides being a gamble for us, Gibson Insurance Agency would also be taking a big risk. I wasn't sure if Greg and the partners would be willing to do this. Kimra and I talked and set what we felt was a reasonable floor for what we would be willing to accept to make the jump. I had not shared this with the Gibson people.

I still remember getting the email from Greg. I looked over at her, took a breath and muttered, "Here we go." I began to read through the email as she looked at me intently. "Well? What does it say?" She commanded more than asked. They hit it. Exactly. Sure it would be a sacrifice but this move was about more than money.

I dismissed any concerns as I focused solely on the fact that the big stuff was all in order. I was certain I'd be able to teach these folks in northern Indiana a thing or two about the insurance brokerage business. With my trophies and awards in tow, and major overconfidence in my abilities and experiences, I packed my bags and came back home to Indiana.

Chapter One – Leadership Lesson

Liz Misenar, Principal at Gibson

Liz joined Gibson in 1993. It was her second job out of college. She runs Gibson's Business & Private Client Group.

Strong Foundation
Gibson was technically my second job after grad school but it was my first real career move. I joined the organization in the mid-90s after being completely disillusioned by a very short stint at a competitor. Gibson was everything I thought my first job should have been – **cutting edge, flexible, great culture, and VERY results-driven**. If you had the results, you got the reward! Incentive bonuses were paid at year end and were tied directly to results.

Dave Gibson told me "with results comes freedom" but I was so busy trying to figure out *what* I was doing and *how* I could get results that I wasn't sure what "freedom" I could have possibly earned. We worked hard and no other competitor outworked us. It was almost a badge of honor.

Culture of Innovation
I remember the intense push to look outward for new ideas and competitive knowledge. **Leadership was active in various roundtables, company advisory councils, and affiliate groups.** We were encouraged to network with our peers and generate new ideas or improve on existing ideas.

Dave was an idea machine! I remember one of my first official meetings with him as the newest manager. He threw so many ideas at me I must have looked like a deer in headlights.

Changing of The Guard
When Dave realized a **new leader was needed to continue our success**, he passed the torch to his second-in-command, Greg Downes. **It felt seamless to me.** Results were still demanded and under Greg's direction, I was starting to understand how I could make an impact. We had

several Best Practices Awards under our belt and we were soon awarded with several local and state Business of the Year Awards. We were also featured several times in national industry publications. Each year, sales were better than the year before and profitability was at an all-time high. We had a tremendous reputation for technical expertise, professionalism, and working hard for our clients.

Feeling Comfortable – Too Comfortable
We all really felt **we had this figured out**. We knew the market swings and how to play the game. Sure, a few business units weren't growing as much as our Executive Leadership Team thought they should be, but they were seeking out new talent to make that happen. We all had great confidence in their ability to move us forward.

Enter Tim. I remember thinking what an impressive hire, but why would this guy want to leave Arizona to come here? I had no idea at the time what impact this would have not only on our organization, but especially for me. I am now a partner leading a business unit. Our organization was about to change in so many ways but I'll let Tim tell the rest of this story.

Chapter 2 – The Letter

The first six months at Gibson were a blur. We retooled the employee benefits division. While we didn't have the right sales talent, I was pleasantly surprised at just how good our service team was. Executive leadership was very supportive of all that was going on. I stuck to my familiar script from nearly a decade of work in employee benefits and before long had the sales and service teams energized and growing rapidly.

I didn't realize right away the silos that had been forming in the organization, starting with the language we used. We called our practice areas and business units "divisions". In all I think our 75 employee company had around 10 divisions. And divided we were.

Standard Operating Procedures were highly valued at Gibson. Right down to the paper sign out log at the front desk or how and when to use the Do Not Disturb (DND) button on your phone. I had never been anywhere that invested training time on these things. And certainly not where that was seemingly more valued than results.

We laminated posters and hung them in the break rooms and above copy machines with sayings like, "Have you DND'd today?" In fact, some self-appointed "DND Police" would report my violations to Greg. At one particular meeting of all my peer managers (which I showed up late to) Greg pounded his fist on the table while angrily addressing me for the poor example I was setting and the extra work I was causing for the receptionist when my phone was left off DND.

We were moving at warp speed in my division and having great success. Never before had our company had such significant new business sales results. I was working ten and twelve hour days and admittedly didn't always remember to push the DND button on my phone. I of course didn't see it as a big deal. The reality was that this was just one example amongst many where I was bypassing and trampling on years of "how we've always done it."

Nearly every week would bring some type of interaction with my peers that included small minded or shortsighted behavior in my view. I would roll my eyes and scoff when I observed it. I was literally in disbelief.

By the end of 2006, the honeymoon was over. In my division, although we were growing like crazy, we were also contributing mightily to the surge in expenses with additional staff and resources. As a company, revenues were slipping as the other divisions had completely stalled. Costs had been soaring as we brought more people on throughout the organization in anticipation of future planned growth.

Thanks to Gibson's highly formalized review process, cracks in my personal armor began to appear. My peers in the other divisions didn't appreciate my absent reverence for the past, or the additional investments and resources the company was allocating to my area. They fairly criticized me for lacking an overall perspective of our industry as I leaned on my background running a specialty practice like employee benefits. Likewise I didn't understand their lack of regard for the results my division was experiencing. What could matter more? Apparently pushing the DND button.

It was at this time, in December of 2006, that Greg Downes gave me a copy of Pat Lencioni's book *Silos, Politics and Turf Wars*. I was mildly familiar with Lencioni's work and had read *The Five Dysfunctions of a Team*. Greg's inscription read:

JIM

WITH ALL THE INCREDIBLE SUCCESS WE'VE ENJOYED IN BENEFITS SINCE YOU JOINED US, TURF WARS ARE VERY LIKELY TO DEVELOP. TOGETHER WE CAN MAKE SURE THAT NEVER HAPPENS. KEEP UP THE GREAT WORK!

GREG
12/06

I appreciated the book and his encouragement. But two thoughts came to mind. One was that I had no time to allocate to reading a neat little fable. And two, I wasn't the one that needed to read this particular book. It was many of my peers and colleagues. I kindly thanked him and put the book on my shelf, where it would stay for a few years.

As we rolled into 2007, the small fights became big ones. Weekly, if not daily, battles were happening amongst division managers and even partners. Some was out in the open but much of it occurred in closed door meetings. Somehow it even drifted into salespeople vs. the service teams (which I had never been associated with before in my career).

There was much back channeling and manipulation going on. I was right in the middle of much of it. However unlike those I was struggling with,

I wasn't beholden to years of tradition or hierarchy. I had given up a lot to come to Gibson and wasn't going down without a fight.

My frustration boiled over after I became a partner in January. I was now on the inside and privy to a much fuller but alarming view of our future. In terms of our independence being viable over the long haul, we were in an even tougher position than I imagined. All of my hopes and dreams about Gibson, all the reasons I moved my family from Arizona back to Indiana, all the friends and colleagues we left behind, all the motives to give up a lucrative role running a thriving practice with a major national player were slowly but surely fading into a festering disappointment.

Although my division was growing rapidly, the institutional inertia present in Gibson was threatening to keep our company on a path to mediocrity that would inevitably lead to slow decline and selling out to an aggregator. I was getting nowhere trying to convince the other partners that we needed to quickly and radically change in order to survive. The substantial personal financial investment my wife and I had made was already underwater. It was looking like my gamble on Gibson would be a bust. It literally made me nauseous.

My 18 months at Gibson were barely a blip on the radar screen as compared to our veteran employees. We were blessed with a number of very tenured people. Some began working for us in our Plymouth, Indiana, office right out of high school. Every year several were celebrating milestone anniversaries - 25, 30, 35 and even 40 years - with the company. I was the antithesis of this.

We were in many ways a great organization, known for integrity and family values, and in the midst of planning a major 75th anniversary gala for the following spring. Yet there were sizeable fractures developing in our foundation. As an organization we weren't able or didn't want to admit that maintenance was desperately needed before it reached a point of no return.

Publicly the other partners had been unable or unwilling to take a strong and sustained stand in various forums – manager meetings, partner meetings, etc. In private, some of them acknowledged they shared my concerns but had lost hope in their ability to influence our direction.

Others just couldn't see the path that we should take. This did give me some faith that it was worth it to continue the fight.

In my mind things were so obvious. We weren't moving fast enough. We were missing the opportunity to become great due to stubbornness, clinging to old and "safe" ideas and a lack of resolve. Even though I had just proven that we could take a big practice area within the company and retool it on the fly with significant growth, no one wanted change in *their* area. Good had become the enemy of great.

It finally reached a point where I knew I had to choose between taking action or moving on from Gibson. The idea of giving up sickened me and I decided I had no choice but to take a strong stand without regard for the personal consequences.

I kept thinking about what I could do to draw attention and serious dialogue to our concerns. It was so important to get the topic out in the open where we would all be forced to take a public stand on our commitment to remaining independent. For me, everything was at stake.

But who would have the stomach to make the hard choices that independence required? The regular structure of our stockholder meetings didn't leave a lot of opportunity for a conversation of this magnitude. And Greg didn't seek it out from those most disenfranchised.

We needed something to spark the conversation. After much thought, a compelling and candid letter to my partners seemed like the best tool I had. I figured it would take a few weeks to craft the letter. I ended up writing the rough draft in one night.

The day before sending it out, I asked Greg, our CEO at the time, to read a draft of the letter. I told him that out of my tremendous respect for him, I would not send it without his permission.

Greg wrote an email back to me: "Tim, all good questions and relevant points, and I take no offense at any of them. I welcome the dialogue and wish that more of the partners would speak up when given the opportunity. Unfortunately, that rarely happens." So, out the letter went.

As Kimra and I drove to the airport that afternoon of May 15, 2007, we looked at each other several times but said nothing. Finally she broke the silence. "What do you think will happen?" I understood by the way she asked the question, that to her this was about more than what would happen at Gibson, but rather what would happen to me. As in, would my fellow partners at Gibson desire to keep me, and by virtue "us" around?

To My Fellow Gibson Partners:

- **We need to be more agile.** *One of our strengths as a small, closely held company should be our ability to react swiftly to challenges and opportunities. We should be quick and nimble, outflanking the "big boys". We have essentially taken one of our greatest assets off the table.*

- **Our value proposition seems a little stale.** *Do we provide a unique service or resource? Do we have special industry experience that can only be found at Gibson? If our value proposition is not winning consistently enough against our current competition, what is going to happen when the competition improves?*

- **We are inwardly focused and intoxicated by our past success.** *Do we know how we stack up versus today's competitors? How are we being sold against, and what is driving our competitors' success?*

- **Too many in our organization undervalue how we got to where we are at.** *We have become openly disrespectful to some of our salespeople. We need to stop the notion that every deal is a robotic transaction that will come to fruition with the right script or policy and procedures manual.*

- **We have the culture of an insurance agency versus a sales organization.** *Are we an insurance agency first, that needs to sell things once in a while to survive? Or are we going to be a professional sales organization, first and foremost; and what we sell just happens to be risk management advisory services?*

- **We have a top down approach to management.** *Input from key individuals is not sought in the early stages of formulating important* *new initiatives. As we continue to groom and look for the future leaders of the organization doesn't it make sense that we begin to seek their input early on? Why wait until they're a manager or a partner to push them for input. Creativity and passion spurs growth. Are we taking advantage of this?*

- **We need to have the courage to confront.** *Stating the truth and providing constructive feedback is not mean. It's necessary. We must begin to hold ourselves and others accountable.*

- **We need to settle the issue of perpetuation.** *We're in a state of suspension as an organization. We're not going anywhere (which means we're going backwards). We are lacking a clear vision of the future. The questions of organization, leadership and talent perpetuation need to be settled. It's not just a matter of trying harder or needing more time.*

- **We are on the threshold of a crisis.** *I truly believe that if we don't decisively act upon these key issues in short order, we will set into motion a series of actions that at best will not keep us independent and at worst could have serious financial consequences for us as partners.*

When our plane landed in New York later that day, I naively expected to see a number of "reply to all" emails stating firm agreement with the points I had raised. Instead I got the email version of crickets. It was beginning to feel awfully lonely. I wondered if I had overplayed my hand.

Although I received some private and public responses of support, one public reply probably summed up how many of my fellow partners were feeling:

I have to admit after the first read-through I was thinking 'Wow, Tim, is there anything we do right in your opinion?' and 'Give us a break, how do you think we made it where we are without you?' On the second read-through I realized I was reacting to the communication style vs. the core issues/concerns. I would like us to meet as a group to discuss these in person vs. via e-mail or in individual side bar conversations.

This translated in my head to, "Upon reading this carefully it's hard to argue against it but you're a real jerk." This comment and others like it – even if they weren't worded quite as strongly – definitely stung.

On one hand, I appreciated how they felt. I wasn't reverent to our history or traditions. The style I chose was aggressive and incendiary – not very "partner like". On the other hand, I felt like a bit of martyr. I was doing the badly needed dirty work that no one else had the stomach for yet being dinged for style points.

One thing was definitely true. The confrontational approach I chose wasn't an accident. It was driven in part by the arrogance I still carried having very successfully run a large practice in a big city for a public company. Alternatively I'd preferred to tell myself that it was 100% necessary. Without some type of major provocation or catalyst, the commitment for change by my fellow partners wouldn't come fast enough.

I felt we were on a giant chess board and had more pieces left than our opponent. Naturally most in the audience felt we were winning. The only problem was that somehow I was seeing the board eight or nine moves ahead and realized how close we were to a checkmate. I couldn't get this thought out of my head and certainly wouldn't allow myself to stand by and let it happen.

Over the coming months our partner group would debate whether we were truly "on the threshold of a crisis". Greg opportunistically utilized the letter to spark change in our organization.

Some things would require revolutionary change. We had to move boldly and quickly or we would miss our closing window of opportunity. Others issues required a steady and more patient approach. We would use the tremendous building blocks of our past to evolve for the future.

> *We would use the tremendous building blocks of our past to evolve for the future.*

Little did *we* know that the Great Recession was right around the corner. It would actually be the final push we needed to implement our overhaul. Little did *I* know just how trying the next several years would be for me on a personal level. I would have to evolve, too. As Greg often said when referencing leadership, "The skills that got me the job weren't the same ones I needed to do it well."

With that one click of the send button, the beginning of our journey was set into motion. We would be retrofitting Gibson on the fly over the next few years.

Chapter Two – Leadership Lesson

Tony Hutti, CEO at Renaissance Executive Forums Indiana
Tony runs several CEO roundtable groups in Indiana. Both Greg Downes and Tim Leman participated in Tony's groups for a number of years.

Courage Needed
Every executive must make a decision or **take action that requires courage**. The action by Tim Leman to write the letter and decision by Greg Downes to allow it to be published, reminded me of President Kennedy's *Profiles in Courage*. The book profiles senators who defied the opinions of their party and constituents to do what they felt were right. **Courage in business and life is becoming more critical with the velocity of change**.

Change Is Inevitable
There are several disruptive technologies and a shrinking world that have and will challenge executives. For Gibson they were:

- Changing their business model due to changes in the marketplace
- Accepting the truth about the long term outlook of their company, even as the market leader
- Transitioning from a "command & control" leader to a collaborative one
- Challenging peers to alter the old and adapt to the new

In my coaching work I see it all the time. **Executives must become more adept at initiating change**

Conflict Acceptance
One of the vital ingredients for an executive and a team is **the ability to face, learn, and grow from conflict.** This is the second dysfunction according to Patrick Lencioni. Many executives have a desire to preserve artificial harmony. This stifles open discussions and results in poor or no decisions. One of the crucial leadership traits of Greg Downes was his ability to encourage and manage conflict. This was vital to Gibson and will be even more so for any company to thrive in the future.

Collaborative Leadership

Engaging in open discussion was critical to Gibson's transition. This will become increasingly important as boomers retire and the younger generations step into leadership roles. Collaborative leadership engages both Gen "X" and Millennials **resulting in clearer strategies and quicker execution.**

Chapter 3 – Transitioning Into Leadership

The letter had created quite a stir. Things were getting a little uneasy amongst our group. Greg decided we needed some outside help and hired a consultant to help facilitate feedback and a meeting around the issues raised in my letter. In particular, the final point about labeling our situation a crisis seemed to stir the most angst.

> *Labeling our situation a crisis seemed to stir the most angst.*

Our consultant created a survey for our partners. It was very straightforward. It had two questions:

1. Would you describe Gibson as being in crisis or on the threshold of crisis?
2. If yes, what indications do you see? If not, what indications are there that it is not?

The response from our partners to the "crisis question" was four saying "yes" and nine saying "no". Comments included:

Yes; our stock price went down in 2006. It will go down again in 2007. And the 2008 pipeline doesn't look good. Crisis doesn't mean "going out of business". It just means being sold (no longer independent). We are on that track without changes.

No; but at higher risk today than 5 years ago due to business climate, lack of new business and poor retention.

No; not in crisis because of the stable performance and reputation of organization. Individuals continue to show professionalism and respect toward others. Managers are capable and still value the organization and people within the organization.

No; I do not believe there is a crisis, in fact, I believe for the most part the Divisions are operating quite well. The fact that we are having this meeting here, today, and discussing some of the critical issues as well as forming "subcommittees" to also address critical issues is a huge step in setting the stage for the future direction of the company.

No; issues brought forth aren't insurmountable and have been raised before and we've gotten through them successfully.

When it came right down to it, we were talking about changing 75 years of legacy and culture. We had actually been pretty good as an organization. You don't survive that long without doing something right. And we *had* done it well. We had never stopped doing great work for our clients. Besides the most recent couple of years, we enjoyed a long track record of financial success. So for a newcomer like me to brashly label the situation a crisis didn't feel very good to the others.

One of my senior partners did tell me he felt the same way I did on many of the points in the letter. However he had "become resigned to the fact that he couldn't drive change" throughout the entire organization. "I felt misunderstood whenever I brought similar issues up in our partner meetings," He told me. "After a while I just didn't feel like my opinion mattered."

Throughout our meetings with the consultants my emotions ranged from great excitement to anger and even sadness. When I watched my partners participate in forward looking conversations and acknowledge some of our big issues, I felt inspired and proud that I had sent the letter out. They had taken it to heart and responded to my challenging style. They were engaged and focused on the long term success of the company. This was because success meant the continuance of our legacy: for our clients, our employees and our community. This mattered more than anything else to all of us.

Other times I would begin to boil over inside as I watched the consultants allow the discussion to sway back to a very careful and slow moving process. Calls for more discussion of the issues or formation of committees to study the concerns made me feel they didn't fully understand just how difficult of a situation we were in.

The debate would carry on. My anger subsided but was replaced with a sense of loneliness. After everything that had just happened to our group why didn't the others share my passion? I was on the verge of going to the worst place possible for me. That happens when I stop fighting. In an ongoing and drug out conflict, after repeated attempts at change where I sense no interest in compromise or movement, a pragmatic and logical part of me takes over. I prepare to move on – from them or it.

Clearly our group didn't agree on what "crisis" meant. I think many of my partners probably felt I was suggesting we would have to close our doors. That wasn't the case at all. What many didn't understand – mainly I think because Gibson was all they knew – was that our way of doing business, how we took care of our clients and especially how we treated our employees would be at stake. They just couldn't believe that outcome was possible so therefore we weren't in a crisis. I may as well have been Columbus arguing the world was indeed round. I felt differently and knew certain results, choices and actions would set in motion an outcome we would no longer control.

Coming out of those sessions with our consultant we agreed that some issues were behavioral or cultural in nature while others related more to strategy and client deliverables. They included:

- Improved value proposition for clients
- Higher expectations and accountability for our sales team
- Increased focus on growth
- Faster implementation of new initiatives
- More inclusive leadership and decision making

While there was consensus around the issues, progress in addressing them felt slow to all of us. I began to realize that even when we all wanted to turn our ship around, it wasn't easy. We couldn't agree on the direction. It was a difficult spot for me. There was some

> *I began to realize that even when we all wanted to turn our ship around, it wasn't easy. We couldn't agree on the direction.*

movement and it gave me just enough hope that I hung in there. But it couldn't come quickly enough.

I was dialed into growth. Without it, I knew we wouldn't survive in our present form. That meant we would need to marshal all available resources to support growth. It had to be the priority throughout the entire organization and trump other important but less urgent issues.

Alternatively some of my peers felt that we needed to fix our operations first in order to support the growth. I understood their thought process. It made sense. However we didn't have a year or two to make the fixes.

> *We didn't have a year or two to make the fixes.*

At the rate we were going, we would miss our window and be forced to consider selling the company, and with it control over the things that mattered most to all of us.

Additionally others were so far engrained in their particular silo that any type of reallocation of resources – even if best for the organization – was met with stiff but illogical resistance. I tended to write them off as a lost cause.

In spite of this, I forged ahead by focusing squarely on "things" that needed updating and fixing. As Pat Lencioni writes about in *The Advantage*, I took a traditional approach and dove into strategy, marketing, finance and technology. I didn't know it at the time, but I had miscalculated how important the people side would be to our progress.

As a "reward" for speaking up the loudest (and with so many of these initiatives focused on client retention, new sales and overall growth) I was named to the newly created position of Chief Growth Officer (CGO) on January 1, 2008. Greg's internal announcement outlined the new role. In addition to continuing to grow my own book of business, I would be responsible for:

- Setting the direction and achievement of all of our business development activities and production plans
- Leadership of the entire sales team
- Recruiting, coaching and mentoring of sales team members in all divisions.
- Become a member of the Executive Leadership Team, as well as the Board of Directors

I was more than excited. Early on, my enthusiasm was generally matched by my former peers in the sales and partner ranks. One of our own finally had a seat at the table!

This would be my chance to do things the "right way" I thought to myself. Ever since I began my career in sales ten years prior, I had been keeping a mental journal of all the things I would do differently if ever truly in charge of a sales team.

THE SALES WORLD ACCORDING TO TIM
- Do what you have to in order to keep your senior producers engaged and productive
- Force new producers to swim, but don't let quality ones sink
- Leverage the strength of a team versus being a lone wolf
- Create an environment where your best talent thrives and is rewarded for superior results
- Set your non-negotiables but allow them the freedom to adapt
- Don't issue corporate edicts without appreciation for individual circumstances

---

It was all very logical to me. Sales and growth is what kept the engine running. Without it, we wouldn't have clients. No clients meant no jobs and therefore no purpose. We were fighting for our survival. Who wouldn't set aside their differences for the greater good? I could name a few!

Once I had an opportunity to explain this concept internally at Gibson, I was certain everyone would be on board. All we had to do was take the shackles of bureaucracy and administration off, and growth would shortly follow. Yes, I was about to liberate everyone and they would love me – or so I thought.

Chapter Three – Leadership Lesson

Brad Serf, Principal at Gibson
Brad has been at Gibson since 2002. He leads the Construction Practice.

Audacity personified

First Tim's letter and then suggesting that we were fighting for our survival? Some of us were asking, *Does this guy know as much as he thinks he does?* I remember thinking to myself that his approach seemed to show he had little regard for his own future here.

One thing was certain: Tim had earned the trust and confidence of Greg Downes. He was appointed to the newly created role of Chief Growth Officer (CGO). My question was whether he would be able to earn the trust and confidence of the broader group?

During this time, I ran into a former colleague of Tim's from his first job out of college. This gentleman was a long time insurance veteran. He was at one of the national brokers and had tried unsuccessfully to woo Tim to their Indianapolis office. I remember him telling me, "Tim is destined to lead a big company not a little regional firm like Gibson." I couldn't help but take notice of this comment given the source. As I was making up my own mind about Tim, I felt that if a respected leader in the big broker space believed Tim could lead a large firm surely he could lead us. Besides the "sales world according to Tim" was beginning to make a lot of sense to me. I guess for me and some of the other veterans at Gibson we were optimistic but still wondered what the introduction of Tim meant to our roles and future.

Exceptional communication skills

The guy could clearly communicate a vision. Tim talked a good game and had delivered as the leader of our employee benefits practice but would that translate into overall organizational leadership? I remember a meeting with Tim shortly after he took on the CGO role where he explained that my results were unacceptable. On one hand I didn't appreciate hearing that, while on the other hand I walked away with a sense that Tim had the guts to manage and call something as he saw it. The thing is, in spite of him telling me what he did, I left with a sense that I indeed had the potential to improve and contribute in a meaningful way. He saw me as part of the future here. Tim's extraordinary ability to communicate drove much improved rapport with the salesforce.

Proactive

Many of us thought the existing Gibson culture – which had produced good results for 75 years – would again one day produce results. We just needed to stay the course and ride out the recent misfortunes. Tim had developed an organizational awareness that suggested otherwise. While many of us were influenced by the historical environment, Tim had the courage to be proactive and sought to influence the future environment. Most of us could have never imagined that his strategy would catapult our growth so substantially.

Chapter 4 – From Player To Coach

One thing I learned well in Phoenix was how important growth is to an organization. Many problems can be solved or alleviated by additional revenue. With the letter serving as a blueprint, my focus in the newly created CGO role would be on improving our client retention and adding new ones. We were going to grow our way out of this!

For most of my adult life, success had come quickly. I have always connected easily with others. Friends, classmates and associates typically described me as having a lot of charisma or being quite charming. These skills had always come naturally to me and were likely the source of many behavior issues for my parents in elementary school.

At 23, and in my first job out of college, I grew bored with the training plan after a few months, began making cold calls and ended up landing the largest client in the office. A few years later in Phoenix, I was able to hit the ground running. In fact, even though I didn't start with my new company until August that year, I ended up qualifying for the national sales leader award. By the wise old age of 27, they appointed me to run the multi-million dollar practice and lead 30 direct reports. The bottom line was that I had been blessed with good opportunities, great managers and fortuitous timing early in my career. Patience, however, was not one of my virtues.

There was something else I didn't appreciate during the first few years at Gibson. Every role I had been in, I could personally impact and affect the outcome. Yes, I worked with teams of people and was known as a "people person", but when times were tough or the chips were down, I could press harder and personally influence the outcome. I was driven, motivated, ambitious and sometimes controlling. I assumed everyone else viewed the world like I did.

So I used the "build it and they will come" mentality. At Gibson, I would plug in new tools and resources to build an enhanced client experience and value proposition. Our salespeople would be energized and begin making more calls. Prospective clients would be wowed and before long we'd be growing like crazy. It honestly made a lot of sense to me.

As was my style, I moved quickly and reviewed several of the top web-based data warehouse and content tools in our industry. We would be able to provide clients with deep dive benchmarking as well as great educational content for their employees. We found that our local competitors didn't have or weren't using these tools effectively. This would give us a marked differentiator.

I picked a few them and proposed we move forward. One partner wrote me and said, "The providers you selected lack ease of use in rollout and engagement with our client base." I heard something similar from several others but decided they were just pushing back for the sake of it. Our CFO questioned the return we'd get. I replied that I didn't see how we *couldn't* win. Without any "valid" concerns in my mind, I ordered the implementation to begin.

Several months later our adoption rate was minimal and we had very little traceable revenue to show for our efforts. It was perplexing to me. In our executive leadership team meetings, I pointed fingers at the users. They weren't on board! They weren't trying hard enough! And it's also true that there was a lot of passive resistance to an employee benefits person telling liability insurance and worker compensation veterans what to do.

This pattern would continue over the next six to twelve months. I would dream up and hastily order the implementation of new ideas, tools and strategies. Dollars and time were invested with limited realization. I couldn't figure out why. I had seen these same ideas and tools used with wild success in other markets. I became more and more frustrated that "they" didn't "get it".

It also occurred on the people side. I shot-gunned the recruiting process on a couple of very expensive hires. The signs were there in the personality tests and feedback from the interview notes. Once again, I thought I knew better. Although I heard the feedback, I was so caught up in the ongoing battles that I discounted the advice. It's hard to put a true figure on what these setbacks cost our organization, but it was more than just the salaries and recruiter fees.

I began to question myself. I was not used to spinning my wheels. Nor was I prepared for the lack of reception and interest in my ideas. It was about this time that I noticed that copy of Lencioni's book on my shelf. *"Silos, Politics and Turf Wars,"* Yes, we have those I thought to myself as stared at my copy of the book. I decided reading it wouldn't hurt.

As I read the book, Lencioni's words began to sink in. He couldn't have described us any better. Silos are natural but deadly. We had attempted but failed in efforts to create a common goal we were all chasing. We broke the main goal down into many fragments, each owned by a separate division. With so many autonomous divisions, we had strengthened the silos and created unhealthy competition internally.

> *Silos are natural but deadly. We had attempted but failed in efforts to create a common goal.*

Unfortunately I didn't follow Lencioni's advice closely enough. We needed to build a rallying cry with metrics and key objectives that everyone could understand. I didn't get that the process of creating a rallying cry could help bring us together. Instead I dismissed our ability to be on the same page.

I did take comfort and find inspiration from my reading. If nothing else, I knew we weren't alone. Lencioni's example of silos not occurring in a hospital emergency room because of the life and death nature of the moment did strike a chord with me. We still didn't have enough of a crisis to help push people over the edge. So I went for the easy items.

I pushed through a change in the name of our business units. No longer would they be called "divisions". They were now "practices". Tension between sales and service? Let's change the titles of our service team members to better reflect their talent and role with clients. So we did.

Gibson needed a fresh look and feel to match all the change. I pushed for a major rebranding including development of a new logo. New business cards and marketing materials were created. They looked great but weren't seen as important by our team. In fact they just caused extra work as signature blocks and form letters had to be updated.

I was tearing through years of tradition – trying to singlehandedly create a new way of thinking – and didn't appreciate how this impacted everyone. My communication of the initiatives was often poor and rushed. It wasn't purposeful; it just had to do with my relentless push to move us forward.

Feedback on my aggressive approach was mixed. In general I think there was an excited but cautious optimism about the changes as a number of people appreciated the fresh approach. However one of our managers wrote this in my review at the time:

> *Be open to other ideas and perspectives. Work on not going into sales mode when someone disagrees. It makes people feel railroaded and not heard.*

In an effort to gain support and start getting greater engagement with our sales team, I created the Producer Advisory Council (PAC). It was an advisory board of some of our top salespeople. This morphed into the creation of a Senior Leadership Team (SLT) where five of our salespeople were split off from our manager group and placed into an elevated position.

This was possibly one of the most damaging things I did. And I didn't even realize it right away. Sure I knew it would change who was in charge of certain things, but I didn't appreciate just how deeply this would divide our salespeople and manager group. We lost some people directly or later indirectly out of this. Others were just as upset and stayed but I set my relationship back with them by a couple of years at least. How many people did they influence inside the organization based on their negative personal view of me? I had completely changed the pecking order internally and more importantly how the pecking order worked.

Truth be told, not everything we did during this time period turned out poorly. We had changed our typical monthly sales meetings to Growth Huddles. Much of the discussion was centered on organizational results within our company. We talked about company goals and vision. Given how dependent we are on our salespeople and their client relationships, I wanted to help them gain a better understanding of our operations and business challenges. It was a great way for me to get feedback from them, too.

We implemented a very unique team selling approach and compensation plan. The move to teams would turn out to be a significant differentiator for Gibson and remains so to this day. As one of my partners says, "Teaming is so over-used. It doesn't do justice to what we've created."

Our industry was built on a model of the individual producer or salesperson and one or two administrative people servicing the producer's "book of business". Salespeople built up their book over time and if successful would eventually max out their personal capacity. They spent the rest of their career maintaining the book and reaping the substantial financial rewards inherent in the residual income stream coming off that book.

There are two problems with that model. First, there is no easy or natural way to develop new sales talent. Veterans don't have time to help mentor new salespeople and frankly little financial incentive other than their role as owners in the overall business.

"Most insurance brokers can't figure out any kind of sales management that works. Sales Managers are typically just along for the ride. They have no skin in the game. That model doesn't work," commented one of my partners. "Most of the time, the new producers are left to fend for themselves."

We would go against the grain.

In my first sales role right out of college, I had experienced quick and significant success. My annual production matched and exceeded many of the veterans in our company. I had even won the largest client in the office at age 23. But I was terrified on most days. The constant rejection from cold calling and minimal oversight from others in the office, caused me to question my career choice on a weekly basis. I was disillusioned. Sometimes I would put appointments on my calendar and instead wander the newly built Circle Center mall in downtown Indianapolis just to avoid making calls.

The second issue is perpetuation. After having managed the book for decades, the senior producers tend to build relationships with the clients that are bigger than the organization. When it comes time to transfer those clients to someone else, it tends to put the relationship at risk. Many of the brokers amplify this issue by paying the new producer a greatly reduced level of compensation since they weren't the "original" producer of the business. Essentially the new producer inherits a challenging situation taking over for the veteran and gets paid at about half of the going rate.

Likewise, I had always been bothered during my time at the national broker when a senior salesperson with much knowledge and experience but an inability to continue growing was "put out to pasture." True, their compensation could not remain at the same level if their productivity had fallen, but they still had a lot of value to give.

Just as most of our peers in the insurance industry, we struggled with perpetuating our independence. We *had* to successfully bring on new sales talent. We needed to perpetuate the talent to fuel our growth and we needed future internal buyers of our stock. To do that, they needed mentoring and training. This is the number one reason that companies in our industry reach a point in their life cycle where selling out to a national aggregator becomes the only feasible option.

So we developed our teaming model – one of those items on my world-according-to-Tim list – that married up diverse sales, advisory and relationship management talents under a single compensation plan. Our producers weren't immediately in favor of this strategy. In fact it seemed counter-intuitive in many ways. I worked and worked with our group and promised to personally adhere to the same program for my book of business. I was finally able to convince our largest salesperson and a couple of others to move forward with the concept. We would go against the grain and take the personal risk that came with it.

By design, our typically "lone wolf hunters" would have to collaborate to win, grow and secure the upside that came with it, or risk significant cuts in earned compensation. A tremendous premium was also placed on retaining clients. The generational dynamics that developed from the teaming ended up having a hugely positive impact on morale and helped usher in an era of record new business development that continues today. This was an example of the player-coach role being very influential in a positive way.

Today, our largest producer is wildly supportive of the model. "Most of my peers are sitting around fat, dumb and happy. Not me. I'm out with my team in front of clients and having a ball."

He continued, "We developed a model where compensation is truly shared amongst a team of salespeople which creates a completely different dynamic. You take senior people with the most knowledge and technical ability and instead of becoming a wasted asset, they're paired with newer producers whose main role is to get the senior person in front of more buyers. Since the senior person's compensation is dependent on the junior person succeeding, you can bet they'll make sure it happens."

"There is a real sense of dependency on each other. You have a huge accountability to your team. You don't want to let them down!" He told me.

Those on the outside noticed, too. A regional vice president from one of our insurance companies wrote me, saying, "I have been inside most of the top insurance agencies in the Midwest. Your model is unique and I believe one of the best I have ever seen. It is not only effective at leveraging all of the team members' strengths for effective selling but is ideal in developing critical technical knowledge as well."

"Instead of throwing new people into the deep end and saying sink or swim they are allowed to grow in an effective team atmosphere," he said. "Everyone on the team is committed to each other's success and there is strong and meaningful support. Considering that the team is measured together, there is true support which is not the case in other models."

Another initiative had contributed to our success. Even though I had inadvertently increased the height of our already tall silos by forming the PAC and SLT, they both were helpful to me. Through our regular meetings, I was able to bounce ideas off them and reengage some of our senior salespeople who had drifted away. It was an entirely different approach than what they had been used to. A sense of camaraderie developed as ideas and strategies were shared.

For the first time in a while sales were growing. A number of our salespeople seemed to be gaining momentum. You could literally see and hear their confidence growing. I knew I had made a difference at Gibson through my personal sales effort and lead by example approach with the sales team. We even made it to the finals on a huge RFP for a Big 10 school. We didn't win, but our people realized we could compete at that level. I felt pride as some of my ideas and strategies were taking hold.

Unfortunately nobody was prepared for what was coming next. Greg Downes would describe it as the worst day of his career.

Chapter Four - Leadership Lesson

Greg Downes, Chairman Emeritus at Gibson
Greg joined Gibson in 1980 and held the positions of President, CEO and Chairman of the Board at Gibson during his career.

Success Is About Growing Others
For the first time in his career, Tim's **success depended upon OTHERS** instead of himself. He knew the only way to get out of our current situation was to GROW our way out, but GROWTH depended upon the performance of OTHERS, not on Tim's ability to drive new business. As Jack Welch said, "Before you are a leader, success is all about growing yourself. When you become a leader, success is all about growing others."

You Need A Rallying Cry
In an effort to break down the silos, eliminate politics and end the turf wars, Tim inadvertently created new silos with the PAC and the SLT, mainly because there wasn't yet **"a compelling context for working together"**. Even though Divisions became Practices, position titles changed, we had a new logo and rebranded our company, there was no rallying cry, much less metrics and key objectives.

Chapter 5 – The RIF

We were showing signs of life and I was feeling more confident about our direction. In fact when my brother very spontaneously asked me if I would join him on a two week barnstorming tour of Europe scheduled for September of 2008, Kimra strongly encouraged me to go. She knew I needed it.

> *We were showing signs of life and I was feeling more confident about our direction.*

She saw how the past few years had worn on me and considered it a well-earned reward for my efforts. I protested about it being busy season and how I felt I needed to be in the office. "When are you going to have another opportunity to do something like this with your brother?" she asked. Thankfully she won and I booked my travel.

On September 24, 2008, I had dinner with a friend from the insurance industry at a steakhouse near O'Hare airport. He asked how business was going and balked at my very balanced assessment. He talked about how impressed his company was with the positive changes at Gibson. "C'mon, no one has done what you've done in that market!" He exclaimed.

Afterwards he took me to the airport and dropped me off for my redeye flight. As I made my way inside the airport, I was relaxed and reflecting on all praise he had just conveyed to me. I met up with my brother inside and we left for Munich, via Frankfort.

Just five days into our trek across Europe, the Great Recession officially struck. My brother is an investment advisor. His clients began calling almost immediately. Call after call came in. The remaining days were very tough on him. You can see it in the pictures and video of our trip as there is a marked difference in his demeanor before and after September 29, 2008.

I remember feeling bad for *him*. While I knew it was a global event, I didn't fully appreciate how it would impact us at 130 South Main Street in South Bend, Indiana.

A big part of our client base is located in Elkhart County, Indiana. It has been home to the RV and boat industries for a long time. It was also one of the hardest hit by the recession. Unemployment in the county, where we have a majority of our business, led the nation at one point. President Obama visited four times in a 15 month period. In one such speech during August 2009, he had this to say:

> *"The Elkhart area has experienced the second greatest increase in the rate of unemployment in the country – up 10 points in a year. It's an astonishing statistic. And there have been times where nearly one in five people in this area have been looking for work. You've seen factories close, and your sons and daughters moved away in search of jobs and opportunity. So this is more than an economic crisis. This goes to the heart and soul of a community. It tests the strength of families and the spirit of good people – hardworking folks who've given their all to a company and now don't know where to turn."*

Just as we were gaining traction, right when our outlook was improving, our revenues began to slide. Profits tanked and we ended up running a negative operating margin for the year. The fees and commissions we generated weren't enough to cover our expenses, let alone make a profit.

I remember my CFO sounding the alarm first. He had been working on our budget forecast for 2009 and came down to my office to let me know. He was solemn when he began to explain just how bleak the picture looked to him. Not only were expenses projected to be up but estimated revenues were way down as the local manufacturing industry and everything dependent on it – the bulk of our client base – came to a screeching halt.

We had some serious obligations to contend with. Beyond the normal operating concerns was our financial perpetuation. We owed sizeable payments to a few retiring stockholders for the equity they had owned in our company. Additionally many of our newer stockholders had aggressively purchased large amounts of stock during the early part of the decade when results were so much better. The projections had many of them upside down and unable to make their payments.

Things were getting dire in a hurry. Our people costs accounted for 70% of our expenses. The only way to dramatically lower our spending was through reducing our headcount. But no one on the executive leadership team could stomach the thought of cutting jobs. We had never experienced mass layoffs or terminations due to economic conditions. To speak of it almost seemed like blasphemy. Gibson wasn't that kind of company. Yet the forecast for 2009 would leave us unable to cover our expenses for the second year in a row. There wasn't a good answer.

We debated and brainstormed on how we could cut our expenses to meet the significantly reduced revenue projections. We froze wages throughout the company and cut our executive compensation. Greg led by example every step of the way. But it still wasn't enough.

We reluctantly agreed to identify some jobs that we could live without. In the end we didn't have any other options. Cutting our workforce was the only way we could remain viable for the survivors. Ultimately we all agreed we had an obligation to the organization and the remaining employees.

> *We had an obligation to the organization and the remaining employees*

It was going to hurt badly for those impacted. There was no getting around it. The best we could do would be handling it in the most gracious and professional way possible. And that's what we did. We made arrangements for severance and career counseling.

My fellow partners were disturbed, too. There were clearly mixed emotions when we told them of our decision at a stockholder meeting. Personal stories abounded about how we couldn't do this, but in the end they understood.

One of them wrote me later saying, "When the RIF was announced my first reaction was one of great sympathy for the employees who were impacted. Knowing the culture and history of our company I knew the pressure on our financials was significant and Leadership would only have done this as a last resort. Honestly, I worried that the initial RIF may not be the last. It was a very unsettling time."

For the first time in our 75 year history we had a Reduction In Force (RIF). It amounted to about ten percent of our workforce. It was gut-wrenching for all of us. For Greg, I think it took a little something out of him that he never got back.

I had much experience over the years with letting people go for cause, but never for economic reasons beyond the employee's control. I sat beside Greg as he started in on a well prepared script. Tears often came next as a feeling of shock and helplessness overwhelmed the employee across the table from us. When it was over, they would leave and we would have a few minutes before the next one. Neither of us said a word. We just sat there in complete silence until the next unsuspecting employee came in. My stomach was in knots.

While the business decision was the right one, sitting across from someone and informing them they no longer had a job was emotionally jarring for me. Greg has told me unequivocally that carrying out the RIF on November 19, 2008, was the worst day of his career. We all knew we had failed our people. I never again wanted to be in position like this.

We followed up the RIF with a hiring freeze and generally operated under the dreaded motto of, "You're going to have to figure out how to do more with less." We cut our education and training budgets to the bone. Only the bare minimum for our continuing education requirements would be allowed. For an organization that prided itself in employee growth and development this sent an ominous message about the future to our employees.

This sent an ominous message about the future to our employees.

Travel and entertainment was also slashed to the bone. We stopped reimbursing for client related mileage costs at the full IRS allowable amount, opting to pay only 80%. And as a symbolic gesture we stopped providing company-paid Kleenex on everyone's desk. Yes, it had come to this. Even the $3 box of tissue didn't survive.

These changes were hard but also so necessary. I felt really helpless because I wanted to personally fix all of it. I knew the best thing we could do for our remaining employees would be to survive until things got better. I became even more motivated to get things turned around. I didn't want this to be my legacy.

As 2008 came to a close my leadership style was being challenged. My main objective – growing the company – was very dependent on lots of other people. Our company was big enough and our client base diverse enough from an industry and geographic perspective, that I no longer had a similar level of technical knowledge as the people on our team. I had to trust them completely to carry out our strategies and deliver our unique client experience.

Additionally the finances for our company were much more complex than running a simple P&L for a business unit. The human resource and employee issues were numerous and also out of my personal comfort zone.

This was a first for me and in stark contrast to being a single salesperson growing a book of business. The very people I was depending on to embrace me had just endured a traumatic series of cost cutting initiatives never before seen in our organization.

Struggling to reach objectives was not something I was used to. The Great Recession had just made things even more difficult in the short run, but it ultimately proved to be another key outside catalyst we needed to begin moving forward.

Another spark would come from my first senior level 360 review at Gibson. It was an annual event for the Executive Leadership Team at Gibson. Anonymous feedback was solicited from the partners as well as the middle management – approximately 20 people in all. There was a numerical section and also an opportunity for comments. It was a knee-buckling experience for me.

My feedback was divided into two camps. Some was very positive; Lots of acknowledgement for the growth in my business unit as well as the whole sales team. Accolades were given for my enthusiasm and energy level. But it was the negative comments I played over and over again in my head.

- *Make sure the SLT has a level of accountability that's appropriate for their level within the organization. It's a slippery slope to take salespeople, make them senior management, give them a considerable amount of decision making authority, yet not have them be accountable to their leadership responsibilities.*
- *Continues to be viewed as someone who has 'favorites' - not that he treats 'others' poorly, but in general doesn't have the same value of 'other' people's expertise & input.*
- *There have been several instances of issues that remain unresolved and the issues are buried under the auspices of "it's being reviewed by the PAC or SLT..." When Tim addressed the shareholders in an open letter a few years ago this is exactly the kind of organizational lethargy he was critical of. Seems that some issues get resolved much more quickly than others, it depends who is being affected.*
- *Tim still needs to make some headway if he's going to be the next President. He should avoid the perception of favoring the sales staff and strive to have positive relationships with all the staff.*

At that moment these anonymous statements were crushing to me. In my head I had just played my guts out and left everything I had on the field. I had done the things that no one else wanted to or could do. Yet I was getting drug through the mud because I challenged a teammate at half time to play harder. Really?

The facts were on my side from my perspective. I remember sinking into a deep funk for several days. Thankfully my wife and a couple of colleagues would help me get my mental state back in order. In one particularly arrogant but candid moment, I remember telling Kimra, "I think they're lucky to have me. Don't they see that everything we've been as a company is crumbling before our eyes? I was asked to grow this place and the main gripe is the manner in which I am doing my job? Growth is the only way out. Nothing else matters!" I was convinced "they" needed to change. Not me.

Through it all she would just listen as I sorted through my range of emotions. She was never combative and always very supportive. She often agreed with what I was thinking but not how I planned to handle it. She counseled me to sleep on it, or in other situations, not respond to a difficult email and instead handle the issue in person. She also reminded me that what might have worked in the smash mouth world of my Phoenix office wasn't going to fly in northern Indiana.

I know it was difficult for her, too. We struggled with what to tell friends and family when they called to see how things were going in Indiana. I didn't want anyone to know that my personal and professional gamble might not pay off. I felt like a failure.

It got so bad one night that she asked the unthinkable, "Well, do you want to leave? We can always move again if that's what you think is best." In some ways I wanted to. I wondered if I was fighting a losing battle. But I couldn't swallow the thought of quitting. It just wasn't in my blood.

Something just kept gnawing at me. What if it was *me*? What if I wasn't as good as I thought I was? That was actually becoming quite apparent. Although unable to admit it to anyone else, I was doing a lot of soul searching. And I was fortunate to have such great support at home.

Chapter Five – Leadership Lesson

Margaret Hartsough, Senior Client Manager at Gibson
Margaret has been a part of the employee benefits practice at Gibson since 1998.

Few decisions could have been more difficult than the Reduction In Force (RIF). To me, the tight-knit team atmosphere that had been championed at Gibson was in direct conflict with the difficult decision of eliminating some of those team members. It was painful for most of us to reconcile the two.

The RIF brought into focus how the economy had truly impacted Gibson. **It was difficult, but it had to be made to avoid even tougher decisions in the future.** I guess it really demonstrated that we were not immune to the recession and the destiny that many of our clients had experienced. That reality suddenly became vivid for those of us who weren't involved in the day-to-day financials of the company and had not seen it coming.

In the days that followed, optimism was scarce but the client work had to be done. It served as a nice distraction. Thankfully the many other changes that followed would bring better times to come, much better times.

For Gibson, our **willingness to change was never more important**. The courage to go through with the RIF was the spark for many transformations. Coming out of it, we streamlined our rigid and often redundant standard operating procedures while bringing more meaningful value to our clients.

Sometimes tough decisions just have to be made, and carried through. At the time, it seemed that all the spirit that had been the heart and soul of Gibson, fled the room. In retrospect that triumphant spirit was never stronger and the new vision Tim had laid out for the future of our organization was never more important.

Chapter 6 – Breakthrough

It was 2009 and begrudgingly I was coming to the realization that I would have to modify my approach if we were going to achieve the kind of success we were capable of as an organization. It was one of those times where you can win the battle but lose the war. What good was it for me to be "right" on a given tactical issue or even a strategic initiative only to have limited buy-in from our team?

Greg Downes was once again particularly helpful to me. I remember one conversation that went something along the lines of, "At some point in time Tim, you will have to make it your responsibility to get them all on board. Take ownership. It's your problem, not their problem."

> *"Take ownership.*
> *It's your problem,*
> *not their problem."*
> *~ Greg Downes*

He was right. I slowly began to stop blaming others for not being in sync with me and made it my issue to bring them along. The forceful model of leadership wasn't going to cut it. I just didn't know exactly how to do it.

I also began to realize that just because something worked for me didn't mean it would for other people. One example was my history of being in a "player-coach" role where I was leading a team of salespeople while also managing my own clients. I just assumed and expected that this type of format would work for others, too. Instead I ended up putting some of our top salespeople into part-time management roles that didn't have them doing what they do best – working with clients. The results were predictable with lots of frustration and slowed momentum.

I was fortunate enough to reconnect with an old friend and mentor, Steve Pahl. Confused, frustrated and at a loss to understand why I was having so many challenges, I gave Steve a call.

At his direction I began reading and then reviewing with him two fairly scholarly books on leadership. They wouldn't be found on the *NY Times* best seller lists and I was less than thrilled about digging into them. But after asking him for help, I didn't have much choice but to follow through. They turned out to be very meaningful in my evolution as a leader.

In Bill Drath's *The Deep Blue Sea: Rethinking the Source of Leadership*, I gained a better understanding of how leadership happens. I had been using too much of what Drath describes as Personal Dominance and needed to evolve to into the more inclusive and collaborative principle of Interpersonal Influence.

Leaders that use Personal Dominance have followers that believe their leadership comes from within. It's a quality or characteristic that the leader possesses. Because of this they are the final truth on all matters.

Interpersonal Influence is all about negotiating between leaders and followers. Influence must be achieved and when it is, leadership is occurring.

I also realized that my style was different than Greg's. For most of his career at Gibson, Greg had a very dominant style of leadership. He and Dave Gibson were a great team. Dave Gibson generated a lot of the ideas and Greg would implement and enforce them. Most of the senior managers and salespeople were afraid to challenge him. They learned over the years that Greg would passionately advocate for what he believed in. Unable to "win", they stopped trying to fight him.

Over time, Greg mellowed in his approach yet many of the tenured people had been conditioned not to press him. After all, he knew Gibson inside and out. He had done some aspect of most of the jobs within in the company. And he was anything but an elitist. He took the hardest assignments, allowed no special treatment for his role and our staff loved him for it. Although combative at times, his integrity was unquestioned. He was the rock. So when he addressed our employees, they fully believed and trusted every word. He was the unquestioned and sole leader of Gibson.

Due to the tenure of our workforce at Gibson, most had not experienced any other leadership in their careers but from Greg. So when I didn't do it like Greg, the perception was that leadership wasn't happening. Using influence was natural to me, but the speed at which I was moving, combined with the volume of work, caused me to use personal dominance. Unlike Greg I didn't have the knowledge, experience or history to pull it off.

Then I read Joseph Rost's *Leadership For The Twenty-First Century*. I had always subscribed to the "leaders are born model". Yet Rost cut right into this traditional "great man/woman" concept. He very pointedly says leadership is only happening if:

(1) Influence and not coercion is the driver,
(2) There is a relationship in place between leaders and collaborators,
(3) They are trying to make real changes, and
(4) There are mutual purposes in place between the people.

To me, the influence part versus all the ways he talked about position, title and role not being leadership really stuck with me. Just because it was more efficient to get things done by directing things, I should try more often to think in my head that I don't even have the authority to do what I'm trying to do. I really needed to persuade or influence someone to my point (more democratic). Along the way, I may getter better, more honest feedback and learn something in the process.

I was definitely guilty of not putting in the effort that influence requires. The good news was that I felt confident I could pivot into this mode.

At about this same time in the spring of 2009 we learned we had not been named a Best Places To Work (BPTW) in Indiana. BPTW uses a survey to measure employee engagement. Employees are asked if they feel valued, if they have a clear picture of the future, how well they get along with peers and what they think of their leaders among other things. The best thing that came out of that was the extensive data on how our employees really felt. I learned from BPTW advisors that company leaders play a huge role in these issues. Too often, they said, leaders side-step or don't see their responsibility in this area. They typically want to delegate all this "soft stuff" to HR. I committed to leading our efforts. We had work to do!

I realized that we needed a new vision of the future. The problem I was wrestling with was a previous ten year vision that we had rolled out in 2005 with a nifty name. We had grossly failed to achieve it. I knew in my head the difference between it and the new vision we needed but was afraid I wouldn't be able to articulate it well to our team. The new vision would seem just like the old one I was critical of. The letter to my fellow owners was turning out to be a pretty good accountability partner as it forced me to fine tune my ideas and strategies.

I began a process of getting together small groups of stakeholders to help collaborate on this project.

The concepts from Rost, Drath and my mentor were fresh in my head. A redo of our vision, mission and values was too important to be crafted by one person. I began a process of getting together small groups of stakeholders to help collaborate on this project.

In these small groups I was able to convey some of the concepts and business philosophies that I so strongly believed in. I was able to learn how others felt, as well as how these concepts fit within Gibson. We did some really great work together. And through it, we bonded. Several employees that I previously sparred with on a personal level got to know a different me. And I came away with a new appreciation for Gibson and its 75 years of success.

In August that year, I was named President and officially moved into the long term leadership transition within Gibson. We began to break down what we do into simple and straightforward language. Our culture was beginning to evolve in a positive manner.

On the revenue front, we couldn't seem to catch a break. Revenues were flat at best. There were a lot of ideas and theories and plenty of excuses as to why. We needed additional clarity.

I borrowed a mantra for our sales team from the national organization I had been at. We opened nearly every meeting with a theme and pounded away.

Our job was to:

1. **Keep the clients we had.** Acquiring new clients was tough work and not nearly as profitable as keeping the ones we had. Besides, they were the ones that helped get us to this point. They would have to be our top priority.
2. **Grow those client relationships.** Too often we didn't view our clients through the same lenses they saw themselves. We would help solve one issue but not even discuss our ability to provide a broader, more holistic solution. We could do more for them. Help them even more! And this, too, was much more profitable for the organization.
3. **Get new clients.** We had to nail one and two above, but there was no question we needed new clients as well. This would be hard work, but I was confident our team could do it.

That's it. Keep what you got. Grow your current relationships. And open new accounts.

> *I knew we couldn't go on like this forever. Everyone has a breaking point.*

We were making progress in so many ways, but not moving ahead quickly enough. Sales were actually pretty strong but profitability was still in the tank. We were still completely locked down on spending and I began to have flashbacks to my experience at the national firm. How can you grow if you don't bring on additional talent? Our people were tired and irritated. Things were very fragile. I knew we couldn't go on like this forever. Everyone has a breaking point.

At our quarterly all-company offsite meeting that October, I decided to hit our whole organization with the reality of our situation. But this time I made a concerted effort to put it in a context that everyone could understand and appreciate. "We were and still are a very good company. We have been for 75 plus years," I remember saying. "We just have to make some adjustments or we won't make it in our current form to eighty years."

We talked about what that meant. We weren't going out of business. No, but our ability to perpetuate our independence and unique way of doing business would be in jeopardy. It would likely require us to sell to a national aggregator. That would mean big changes internally. Many of us would still have jobs with the new company, but some of us wouldn't.

As one senior partner said, "I was worried about our independence. If we had to sell I'd feel like my career was diminished to just a paycheck."

That day we discussed our strong conviction that we could provide greater innovation and service to our clients by not selling to one of the large national organizations. It was affirmation to me that despite the hardships they had been through, this incredible group of people at Gibson wanted to carry on. At that moment I felt so honored to be their leader.

Some of our employees contributed a lot to the discussion. They were feeling the same way but had never felt comfortable talking about it. The meeting gave them a chance to do this. Others had grave looks of concern on their face. Compared to the steady hand of Greg, I seemed reckless. I'm sure they were wondering if the "new guy" would be able to help them overcome these challenges, or would he make them worse? It was a fair question.

It was at this meeting we rolled out our new vision statement, mission and freshened up core values. We focused in on our future sandbox. I wanted everyone to know what our plans were and why we had come to this conclusion.

<u>**Vision Statement**</u>
Become a Top 100 Insurance Broker

<u>**Mission**</u>
Protect What Matters Most

<u>**Gibson Core Values**</u>

- **Clients Come First**: They are the reason we are in business.
- **Integrity Matters**: Always do the right thing.
- **Talent Wins The Game**: Develop and support our professionals as the team of choice.
- **Foster Collaboration**: Innovation is achieved through partnering.
- **We Work Harder**: Nothing will work unless we do.
- **Optimism Reigns**: Attitude and outlook impact results.
- **Committed For The Long Haul**: Independence allows us to make an enduring difference.

The more we emphasized our core values, I noted that some of our employees and partners that didn't uphold them became more and more isolated. In fact we lost a few partners over a several year period. None were good fits for our organization long term, but it would put an even greater strain on our internal financial perpetuation model. Our independence depended on a steady supply of future owners and now we had missed out on almost an entire decade of owners.

The still looming threat of being unable to remain independent long term was always part of our strategy and outlook. We had to find a way to foster an environment where we could recruit and grow enough future partners and leaders to perpetuate our independence or we would be forced to look outside for help. This was a serious threat, but wasn't something we had been able to address. It became another key catalyst for our change.

Our CFO and I wanted to improve our employees' understanding of our financial position and continue to build on our culture of transparency.

So we created the Agency Wellness Index or AWI. It was index score that measured the top four key financial metrics in our business. They were new business, lost business, overall revenue growth and operating profit. They were the key drivers of our company's annual valuation report.

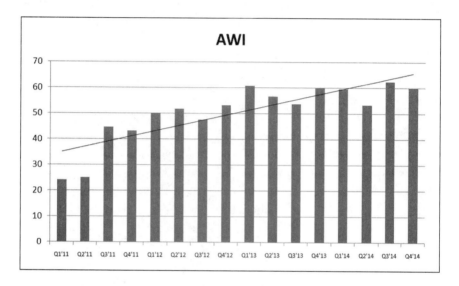

Some details of the metrics were difficult for everyone to grasp so AWI became an easy way for our team to get a monthly measurement of our financial performance. It was all part of refocusing our team on what mattered most to our organization.

We also made a significant move to break up the silos by replacing the individual team bonuses for staff and managers with complete alignment to AWI. Going forward, it would not be about the performance of one business practice or another. We were all in this together.

The offsite meeting with all of our employees turned out to be a success. As coming out parties go, this was helpful to me in my new role of President. Slowly but surely with every meeting or new opportunity to communicate what we wanted to become as an organization, more of our employees got comfortable with the change and with me.

Chapter Six – Leadership Lesson

Steve Pahl, Senior Consultant at Risk Resources
Steve has held numerous positions at carriers and national brokers during his career. Tim Leman got to know him well during his time as the Executive Director of the Gongaware Center at Indiana State University where Steve ran a leadership program.

Leadership: A Dynamic Continuum
Tim's leadership challenge begins with his apt observation that many, if not most, of Gibson's employees recognized leadership as defined by Greg's thoughts, words, and actions. Greg's approach to leadership was most likely formed by what he and many of his generation **recognized as leadership**. That leadership is something a person possesses, imposes on others, and succeeds or fails with. This concept should not be discredited because it has worked and will continue to work. But not for long. Not for the greater number of younger employees and certainly not statically or monolithically.

For an influence model of leadership to work, hiring practices carry even greater weight than they have traditionally because of the relationship that must exist between leaders and followers. Leaders have to be willing to be led by followers. They must acknowledge and embrace the fluidity of influence between those leading and those following. These roles exist in a constant ebb and flow, rise and fall. Not all employees, existing or prospective, are able or willing to take on this mutuality. With existing employees it will become obvious, in a short period of time, those willing and able to 'dance'. New employees are key. How a human resources department identifies and evaluates candidates is a subject wholly separate from this discussion.

It is useful to view the notion of personal dominance and interpersonal influence along a dynamic continuum. Think of Abraham Maslow's Hierarchy of Needs as less of a hierarchy and more of a fluid space. At any point in time leaders and followers must be sensitive to, and act in accordance with, the reciprocal feedback generated during interactions. They must be mindful where each person resides in the continuum and the influence that happens along the journey. This is especially true if a discussion directly affects one's job security and promotional opportunities. The key is to **always listen critically, check for accuracy, and respond empathetically.**

The greatest challenge to interpersonal influence is the ability of all participants to recognize and quickly respond to the constant changes in the internal and external environment. If left unaddressed, it could derail not just the current work but the future and longer range viability of the organization. **Perceived threats to personal and organizational survival may throw the whole dynamic** sharply off course on both continuums.

Chapter 7 – It's About The Culture, Stupid

Throughout 2010, there were more signs of Gibson gaining traction. Yet it seemed that every sign of progress – a significant new client, improved AWI – was also met with an equally significant sign of continued struggle.

The economy was still incredibly difficult. Our region was one of the hardest hit with Elkhart County leading the country in unemployment at one time. In January of 2010 it was still well over 15%.

As was customary, in the spring we received the previous year's company valuation back from our valuation experts in Atlanta. For 2009, our stock price went down again. We didn't know it at the time, but we had bottomed-out as far as our recent history was concerned. The following year we would get a slight bump in value.

We also had tried for the second year in a row to be named a Best Places To Work in Indiana. We missed the mark but gained valuable insight. In spite of what I thought was a very clear vision of the future, it wasn't resonating with our people. At least not enough. The survey numbers proved that.

We had opened up a sales office in Indianapolis a few years prior. It was viewed as a key part of our future growth in revenue as well as a source of future partners and by virtue our independence. I was critical of our plans in Indy, but I had inherited it, and it was now my baby. In spite of my evolving personal view of leadership, I was still in the mode of hiring a "savior" as I felt our only real issue was that we had not recruited the right talent to lead our operation.

At my direction we brought in an expensive search firm. They helped us find and hire an individual from out-of-the area to run our Indianapolis office. He was one of the most expensive hires in our history. At the same time, we had added on some great sales and support talent, including a top college recruit.

All the King's Men couldn't spur on growth in Indianapolis for Gibson – at least not across the board in all business units. We were hemorrhaging cash at exactly the moment we couldn't afford to. We lost a lot of good supporting talent with the lack of strong leadership in Indianapolis, including a close personal friend of mine. I was baffled but parted ways with my expensive hire.

On paper, this should have worked. The candidate had lots of skills and attributes to suggest he could do it. The reality was I had nearly dealt a death blow to our growth plans in Indianapolis. With our need to build a successful operation in a new market, we couldn't afford to be in the spot we were in. Why didn't it work?

A chance encounter with Dave Gibson helped point me in the right direction. He said, "How's Indianapolis going?" Now I knew that we still allowed Dave access to all our financial information online. Dave knew the answer to the question already. He wanted to hear it from me. "Not good," I said. "We just can't seem to catch a break. Nothing's working."

Dave is one of the smartest people I know. I think of him as our very own Warren Buffet. He's also never been labeled chatty. So in his very short style, he replied, "I told you guys you should have sent one of your own down there. It's about transferring culture." And with that Dave walked off.

> *"You should have sent one of your own."*
> *~ Dave Gibson*

The issues in the new office kept eating at me. We were having some success with one of our business units, but not with all of them. And Dave had made it black and white. It was about culture. But how were we going to infuse that into Indianapolis? Believe it or not, the three hour car ride made it challenging.

We ultimately did have one of our younger partners move down to Indianapolis. He uprooted his family and joined our team in Indy. It definitely helped. Over the course of a few years, we were able to pivot and focus our efforts on our employee benefits business which was doing well. It was bittersweet though as we parted ways with some up and coming talent in the risk management side of our business.

Communicating about our Indy office always felt so precarious to me. We had to walk a fine line between the reality of the situation and maintaining an optimistic and upbeat outlook on things. Starting an office from scratch was hard work and something many firms had failed at. I had much better appreciation for that now.

It was a long, slow process but each year brought improved financial results. Most importantly we would learn a number of key lessons that have guided our thinking as we are currently moving into another new market. More on that later.

I wondered if maybe cultural issues were at play in the rest of our organization, too. Could it be the missing ingredient? Was it the reason that we didn't have full buy-in and engagement with all the initiatives? I just had never thought of Gibson as having a culture problem.

What was a better culture anyway? I knew how to treat people right. Even though there was no longer any family ownership at Gibson, we still operated like a family business. In fact, we were probably too nice sometimes. Coddling people more – my view of culture improvement at the time – just didn't feel like the answer.

We also connected for the first time with Larry Linne. As we got to know Larry, I realized he and I had shared a history together in the Southwest as competitors. We studied Larry and the advisory work he was doing with other firms in our industry. We even attended his major peer group fall program in Denver. During the two days at this event, it became clear that he could help us.

Larry had an interesting background. Post-college he played professional football, catching a touchdown pass from Doug Flutie while with the New

England Patriots. Later he would hone his leadership skills as a second-in-command at a construction equipment company.

I knew him during my time at the national broker in Phoenix for his work heading up sales at a large competing insurance broker in New Mexico. Most of our competition in New Mexico could be labeled sleepy but once this "Larry guy" became in charge, almost overnight, their salespeople were out making calls and winning business. Although I didn't meet him personally until years later, I never forgot the impact he had.

More meaningful was the approach I saw at his conference in Denver. We belonged to other peer groups, but none focused on the whole organization the way Larry did. The others typically focused on a product, process or new gizmo of some type that was "guaranteed" to work. Larry passionately called out the leaders in the room to emphasize just how important they would be in any transformation. To Larry it all started and ended with cultural clarity.

Still, after my string of purchasing the "latest and greatest" tools and widgets for our team, without much in the way of results, I have to admit I was worried that signing on with Larry might end up being just another misfire. Candidly I was gun shy. We put the decision to join his group on hold.

My 360 reviews were improving but were still very pointed and somewhat of a mixed bag (much like the rest of our initiatives at Gibson):

- *I think Tim is going to be great. He's got the vision, enthusiasm, and dedication to see Gibson emerge from a very tough economy in a very strong position.*
- *Seems to be doing a good job wearing a couple of different hats. Time will tell just how well he can handle all positions effectively.*
- *It's going to take time for people to trust Tim the way they do Greg. He is a very good sales person and at times it feels like we're getting a sales job.*

Although I had always believed I was a pretty solid communicator, I realized that I still didn't have the complete trust of our team. My skill of persuasion was backfiring with some, as the review comments stated.

I was reading a number of business articles on leaders and communication. Some of the authors spoke of clarity and how it could drive trust. I needed to break things down more often in clear and easy to understand language. And that language needed to be used consistently. I also realized that while I

> *I had to help our team understand what was in it for them – besides just having a job.*

might think I was being clear, there was still much left up to interpretation, starting with our vision, mission and client experience. I had to help our team understand what was in it for them – besides just having a job.

It didn't happen overnight but a seed had been planted. I continued to wonder if the struggles we had experienced to implement what were arguably very good ideas and strategies had a lot more to do with some of this "soft stuff" and less with the idea itself. I just wasn't ready to admit it.

There wasn't any doubt that we were gaining momentum, even with still formidable pockets of resistance amongst our team. I was beginning to know the difference between employees that were not on board because I had not done my part to "reach" them yet and those that had their own personal agendas and weren't aligned with the company. Resistance came in a number of forms, be it how we wanted to run the workflows, to the sales compensation plan, to what we measured and celebrated as a company.

One source of help for Gibson was the economy. By the end of 2010, Real Gross Domestic Product in the Elkhart-Goshen MSA (Metropolitan Statistical Area) had grown by 13 percent, leading the nation. Slowly but surely our clients were recovering. This was a big help for sure.

Just as important were the tough decisions we had made. It left us with improving margins that we used to invest in additional sales talent. We had kept our discipline, even during the lean years, when it came to sales. Now, with employers feeling better about their own future, they began to review all their professional relationships. We had positioned ourselves to gain market share and our producers delivered.

We made a significant change in our ownership structure to address one of our greatest concerns. Losing that batch of partners was a good thing for the cultural health of the organization, but it further clouded our projected ability to perpetuate internally.

In addition to the need to shore up our perpetuation, we needed to do more to engage our employees in more of the detail of our financial health. We had to provide opportunities for them to win when we did well. After slugging through the past 2 ½ years of a virtual lockdown on spending, we needed something to help tell the story and something to serve as a reward for their dedication to Gibson.

I also recalled my time at the national broker. We were a somewhat stuffy London-based public company. A large equity firm took us private in a leveraged buy-out before taking us public again. The power of the IPO as a tool to understand and engage with the full financial picture was intriguing to me.

I had been talking with some business advisors about the concept of broad employee ownership. Very quietly, since 2009, we had been studying an Employee Stock Ownership Program (ESOP). The concept began to catch traction with our partner group. The ESOP could take a minority position and fill the

> *"ESOPs aren't a solution for poor management. ESOPs can't manufacture profits. And ESOPs are not a substitute for a well-run organization."*
> *~ ESOP Consultant*

perpetuation role of the missing partners (without the cultural headaches). It would also meet the goal of engaging and rewarding our employees.

It was not without risk. Our consultant told us we were nearly a perfect candidate for an ESOP. But he warned us, "ESOPs aren't a solution for poor management. ESOPs can't manufacture profits. And ESOPs are not a substitute for a well-run organization."

It also caused anxiety within our partner group. We had a number of healthy debates over several months.

The senior folks were rightfully concerned with how it would impact their major positions within our company. Our newer partners had worked and toiled over the years to (1) be invited, and (2) in a financial position, to become an owner. Some of them felt that suddenly all they had been working toward was now going to be "given" to everyone.

We carefully considered all the feedback and decided to move forward. At the end of 2010 we implemented our ESOP or as we call it at Gibson, the GESOP.

For the first time in several years our stock price stopped sliding. This was a result of improved client retention driven by our service team and some amazing growth in new business by our salespeople.

Our baseline value for the GESOP would be a slight increase in 2010's stock price versus 2009 according to our valuation experts. It wasn't much, but it was up! It felt good to know that someone outside of Gibson had noticed things were turning for the better.

Chapter Seven – Leadership Lesson

Diane Davidson, Operations Manager at Gibson
Diane joined Gibson in 2001 as a Client Service Representative in Commercial Insurance.

Culture is more than just a word

Gibson has always stood firm and proud in its culture. But over the years, the culture had been changing. Long-time employees weren't quite sure what "culture" meant at Gibson anymore, and fresh faces had yet to identify themselves with the culture of the company.

Tim had been making many changes at Gibson. The new Mission, Vision and Values had been rolled out, and it looked and felt different than what we were used to. Most people wanted to believe in it, but there had been some scary times in the not-too-distant past, and it was hard to buy in. Tim was a charismatic leader, there was no doubt, but employees lacked confidence that there was more behind Tim's ideas than just a really good presentation.

I recall Greg Downes sharing the results of an employee survey with the agency early in my career. Although the results were largely favorable, I remember how personally he had taken some of the more "constructive" negative comments. His initial reaction was one of anger: *"Don't these people get it? They clearly just don't understand how committed we are, how much we do for them."* As he stood up in front of the entire employee base that day, he recounted the evolution of his reaction. He had been angry at first, and hurt, and then gradually came to an acceptance. He stated something that resonated with me to this day, **"Perception is reality."**

Tim was coming to terms with this in his own way. It didn't matter what Tim believed, or even what he and his fellow leaders knew, about his ideas. It didn't matter how smooth and charismatic his presentations to the agency were. What mattered was how people perceived it. When people react with distrust, it is easy to assume they just *don't get it*, that they're missing the point, not thinking big enough, not understanding the whole story. But the truth is, their perception is their reality. And as a leader, it is not enough to sweep those perceptions under the rug and discount them as "not getting it". It was time to reach out differently to all the employees, to change their perception, to better define Gibson culture in this new age.

Everyone Matters
When the ESOP was introduced, it was new and confusing to everyone. It sounded good, and even on paper it looked incredible, but there was also an air of distrust surrounding it. Is this *too good* to be true? What are we missing? Why does Gibson want to do this?

As the years have progressed, there has come not only a deeper understanding of the concept of the ESOP, but more importantly a sense of trust in the reasons behind it. Everyone matters at Gibson. New owners are celebrated. There is a sense of unity like never before. Truly, we're all in this together.

Chapter 8 – Battling Instinct
With The Soft Stuff

The positive momentum continued in 2011. Our AWI score was increasing and foretold our future valuation increase, too. Revenues were growing and in spite of the investments we were making, our operating profit had turned positive. Most of the modifications we were making were well received by our team. Change was constant as we tweaked and improved.

My 360 review feedback mirrored the engagement level from our employees.

- *He continues to validate his role as President. Seems to have made an effort to understand the other business units a little better. Has become more constructive in his criticism of others.*
- *Great strides in reaching out to broader employee levels, instilling their trust, powerful company meeting presentations.*
- *Continue to work on instilling trust to entire agency. Has come a long way on this. Continue to develop leadership skills. Improve open listening and take viewpoints of others into consideration.*

In spite of this, that all-too-familiar ache was still there for me. Yes we were doing better, but there was still something we were missing. There was a lot of uncertainty that I had a hard time understanding. Clearly no matter my opinion, my message wasn't resonating with everyone. I quietly wondered if it ever would.

We had stayed in touch with Larry Linne into 2011. In fact he had been promoting his first book entitled *Make The Noise Go Away*. It was about teaching 2nd-in-commands how to keep the 1st-in-commands doing what they do best. We liked it so much, we asked Larry to come speak to a group of our clients.

After hearing his presentation, I became more intrigued with becoming a member of his network. When Larry said he would personally coach me that spring, I decided to move forward with hiring him. Larry and his team promptly performed an overall assessment of our company that helped build a framework for our future success.

By mid-2011 my coaching sessions with Larry Linne moved from the overall assessment and implementation of our value proposition and new business development processes to something I thought was a lot more esoteric in nature. He began to talk about the need for more clarity from me.

That seemed to fit in with my 360 feedback and our annual employee survey. I just didn't know how to go about doing it. I thought I was being very clear in my interactions and conversations with people. Larry's constant push on this topic began to make sense.

I was named CEO of Gibson in June of 2011. Larry would be a big help as I fully assumed the leadership of Gibson. A key point in the recap notes from our coaching session that month was, "Language drives culture. This is the number one thing that Tim can do. Speak the language of what he wants the organization to become."

> *"Language drives culture. Speak the language of what you want the organization to become." ~ Larry Linne*

After our August call he wrote, "Continue to create 'language' to move the culture. However, realize that until everyone is 'thinking' the same way, the culture will not move. You, as the leader must find every opportunity you can to talk about the changes and what you see the future looking like with how Gibson sells, services, and what they offer to clients."

Although the year prior we had recast our vision, it wasn't connecting with everyone. A simple but lofty "Become A Top 100 Broker" just didn't inspire many of our people. They didn't understand what that really meant and how they fit into it. Larry continued to press for clarity on this. I was struggling with the concept of a "statement" that could truly describe all that we hoped to become over the next 10 years.

One of my partners told me recently his memory of our efforts at an SLT retreat to "nail it". He said, "I'll never forget being at Greg's lake house and we had set a goal to walk out of the meeting with the right vision. Hours later we had nothing. Zilch."

Larry helped me break the mental logjam when he said, "Maybe you should think about more of a 'vision paper'. Write out what you want it to look like and see if that helps. How can you possibly fit all that you want to become over the next decade into a couple of sentences?" He wanted it ready for implementation by the end of the year.

Our Vision:

The year is 2022. We are achieving $25 mm of Commission and Fee Revenue, spread among our units the following way:

			$25,000,000
Commercial Risk Management	CRM	45%	$11,250,000
Employee Benefits	EB	40%	$10,000,000
Private Client Group	PCG	7%	$1,750,000
Business Group	BG	3%	$750,000
Workforce Consulting	WC	5%	$1,250,000

Having grown organically with some smaller acquisitions mixed in, we are the largest employee owned risk management advisor in Indiana and Michigan with vibrant operations in South Bend, Indianapolis, Fort Wayne and Southwest Michigan.

The growth in our firm has provided many new opportunities for development and growth for our current team of professionals. New roles and positions have been created. Extensive investments in technology, and collaboration, in and across business units, have made our teams more efficient and effective than ever before. A combination of our employee ownership, steady growth, and the consolidation taking place in the industry has made Gibson a sought after destination for the best and brightest. In fact, the first participants with over ten years in the employee stock ownership plan have begun to retire and take advantage of the additional personal wealth created by the GESOP.

We measure our success by the Agency Wellness Index (AWI), reflecting our achievement versus the prior year in (1) new business, (2) lost business, (3) revenue growth and (4) operating profit. We consistently hit an AWI score of over 65, while sometimes reaching quarterly scores in the 80s. Each operation is achieving the Gibson "Rule of 20"; meaning when the operating profit percentage is added to the growth percentage, it equals 20 or greater.

Our colleagues manage their Personal Brand by living out our Core Values as highly engaged owner-employees.

- ▶ **Clients Come First:** They are the reason we are in business.
- ▶ **Integrity Matters:** Always do the right thing.
- ▶ **Talent Wins The Game:** Develop and support our professionals as the team of choice.
- ▶ **Foster Collaboration:** Innovation is achieved through partnering.
- ▶ **We Work Harder:** Nothing will work unless we do.
- ▶ **Optimism Reigns:** Attitude and outlook impact results.
- ▶ **Committed For The Long Haul:** Independence allows us to make an enduring difference.

We ***Protect What Matters Most.*** This is our mission. To accomplish it we have changed the way risk is viewed in the communities we serve by taking a broader view which includes not only traditional hazard risks, but also business and strategic risks. We exclusively and consistently utilize the **Gibson Protection System (GPS)** to perpetually live out our mission. We leverage a combination of the human capital of our Gibson team and our strategic partners, along with our unique tools and resources, to identify and proactively address existing and emerging risks. GPS is a multi-faceted process including the following:

1. **Executive Briefing:** determines if there is compatibility between our organization and a prospective client
2. **Assessment:** an overall review of the risks faced by the client
3. **Road Map:** provides an overall scoring and snapshot of where the client is initially
4. **Plan:** prioritize our work through a written business plan
5. **Implement:** proactively begin to address prioritized risks
6. **Engage:** infuse our people and processes with their team in an ongoing manner

The success of GPS has elevated our status with our clients to that of key advisor, differentiating us from the traditional insurance agent or broker. Clients regularly tell us and others in the community that we are a key, trusted and indispensable business partner. They rarely make major decisions without consulting us.

Our clients tell us that the **"Gibson Client Experience"** separates us from the competition.

1. **We know them.**

   Our relationship is more than a policy. We know our clients, their people, their industries and nuances, and what matters most to them.

2. **We are their expert guide.**

   As a key, trusted advisor, and indispensable business partner, we are known for our proactive leadership and advice. They value our knowledge and innovative solutions.

3. **We are on their side.**

   We make our clients feel safe, protected, special, valued, and known; and act as their greatest advocates.

Buyers that are uninterested in focusing on what matters most, as well as GPS as a means of solving their issues, are not good fits for our organization. Because of our disciplined approach to maintaining a robust new business pipeline and our commitment to organic growth, we are able to confidently walk away from "opportunities" that do not meet the Ideal Client Profile.

We *GIVE What Matters Most* to our Colleagues, Clients and Communities by using the considerable strength and resources of our organization to improve and assist those around us. Gibson's GIVE provides major training and development opportunities for both our employee colleagues and to the community. GIVE also applies a focused and integrated approach to helping our communities that builds on the knowledge and expertise of our organization and aligns with our commitment to bettering our communities for the long haul.

This ignited a major shift in my thinking. Suddenly, I had real clarity. Can you imagine? As the President, I had helped drive and create a vision for the company just a year prior. Yet, until I went through this exercise, I didn't know that I wasn't fully into it myself. Now I was. I was completely energized and couldn't wait to share my thoughts with Larry. I sent a draft to him in December. He responded:

> *You are the man! This is outstanding. I want to come work for your company. This has refined into the perfect communication of who you are, where you are going, and how you will get there.*
>
> *Congratulations. I challenged you to have this done by year end and you have accepted that challenge and met it.*
>
> *Go OVER-communicate it now. That is the next step and what we will spend time on in our next call. The over-communication model will require your consistency as well as a clear plan of how others will communicate this message throughout 2012 (and beyond).*
>
> *Well done Tim. I know it took a lot of work to get this done. It will pay off with better and quicker decisions and focus from your people.*

I also knew exactly how I wanted to communicate it. This would be like a pre-IPO road show. We would take the message to our team directly with every single employee. I asked to see all of our employees in a small group setting. I think we ran about dozen meetings to accommodate everyone. It was truly a defining moment for our organization and for me.

The same partner who mentioned getting stuck at the retreat added, "Tim, you just took it and did it. The words in the document were great, but the execution was the best part! You had everyone reciting our core values at literally every company meeting or gathering. Knowing how much you believed in it was the thing that made it so inspiring for the rest of us."

Chapter Eight – Leadership Lesson

Bob Sturtevant, Principal at Gibson
Bob has been with Gibson since 1985. He has been a teacher and mentor for many of the risk management advisors at Gibson during his thirty year career.

It Must Be Clear
A leader must be a good "artist" for the organization. Think about a painting that stirs up emotion and passion in its subjects. Isn't it the same? Like an artist, the leader needs to stir up passion for the organization and its employees. Ultimately, the desired result is that people will be creative and go beyond expectation because they are inspired to do so. **The clarity in the vision instills passion, faith and energy.**

To stay the course, the leader needs to communicate and even **over-communicate the message**. I recall vividly when Tim introduced our new Mission and Vision at Gibson a few years ago. He repeatedly energized the staff by having us memorize our core values. Every meeting was started with reciting the core values and mission while providing us with progress reports toward our vision. It became a game and everyone played along. You knew that at the next meeting there was a good chance you were going to be called on! This **over-communication** assured that everyone understood. The picture was clear. The vision was real.

Poet David Whyte writes on the artistry of leadership, "Creating the next great thing demands constant innovation; it's a design task, not merely an analytical or administrative function. Historically, such creativity has been the primary competence of artists, not managers."

A vision is created. A vision is clarified. A vision is communicated. It's the stuff that leaders are made of.

Chapter 9 – Liftoff

With Larry's guidance I was able to bring clarity to our team with our grand vision for the future. We talked about our values and how they snuggly fit into the picture. They were how we would conduct ourselves. We also covered product clarity, our Gibson Client Experience, culture and our brand.

Some of my key staff wondered if I could afford to devote so much time to our vision project. I understood their point, but with each additional meeting, I became rooted in the need to see this process through. And that included keeping the communication up even after the "road show" was over.

The advantages were immense for us and me.

- As I wrote the presentation, I was able to visualize it, understand it and know it. Because it was developed with much collaboration within our team, I knew there would be support for it. This brought me great confidence. While I believed in all of it, the minute I put the words to paper, my conviction became even stronger. We – together as a team – had done a great job with this. It was all so connected and interrelated. It just made sense.
- Our employees saw my unwavering commitment and confidence and became true believers themselves. I had people tell me they never realized what an exciting future we had in front of us! Yes, it would be hard work, but there was an opportunity to be special as an organization.
- It was also one of the acts that completely solidified my role as the leader of Gibson. This was *our plan* and although I had lots of help, I was seen as its chief architect.

- Our people felt "in the know". Always fairly transparent with our team, the vision spelled out how we would win and where we do it. We talked about plans for acquisitions and growth.
- We had a fresh and exciting story to talk about with new recruits. Our campus recruiting began to explode. The recruiting we did in 2012 laid the groundwork for an amazing haul of young talent in 2013 and 2014.
- While remaining flexible, we also had a plan. When opportunities or initiatives came up that didn't fit with the vision, we knew we could set them aside. We were on a mission now!

So while it took a lot of time, just the initial feedback from our employees was enough for me to know this was the tip of the iceberg. I had now become a believer in the "soft stuff". Bringing clarity to my team was a familiar topic in my monthly coaching calls with Larry.

> *I had now become a believer in the "soft stuff".*

I also started meeting with every new hire during the first week of their tenure with us. I walked through our vision, mission, core values and client experience. We discussed their experiences with company culture, what brought them to Gibson and what they could expect.

Once again this was a time commitment, but a valuable one. It served a couple of purposes. Hearing this directly from the CEO showed we placed great importance on it. I strongly conveyed that our core values were not a poster on the wall. They signified what was important and also how the new employee needed to act in order to be successful. Secondly, they became a form of accountability. By so strongly communicating our expectations for them and for ourselves, we didn't leave much wiggle room to be anything but those values. It also seemed to drive a lot of excitement and inspiration within our organization.

In the spring of 2012 we received our valuation for 2011. This would be the first stock valuation since our baseline with the GESOP. We all held our breath a little. Our experts did their analysis and determined an 8% increase in company value. We were back and the timing couldn't have been better!

Larry continued to work with me and our leadership team to expand our thinking with regards to what our clients needed. The concept of emerging risks and therefore emerging strategies took root.

We were asking our salespeople to broaden the definition of risk and as such the ways we could help our clients. While I felt we had always done a lot more than place an insurance policy, Larry was challenging us to see our clients' world through a different lens. Doing this successfully would be no small task. We were talking about turning the traditional model in our business upside down.

I had concerns about how quickly and how much these concepts would be adopted. Fresh in my mind were some of the other "good ideas" we rolled out to our team with minimal adoption. But something was different this time. With the foundation of our vision in everyone's mind, we began to change and evolve our process at rates I had not seen. Instead of a management initiative, it was adopted by the sales teams as their process. They worked together to tweak it and make it better. They owned it.

As the speed of our adoption increased, I continued to gain confidence in our ability to make more changes. We had been playing defense for the past three years or so. Now the wind was in our sales and we were ready to go.

There is no doubt that it was a lot of hard work. But I have to tell you that I loved every minute of it. I saw every session, every meeting and every conversation as a chance to continue as our Chief Vision Evangelist. My reviews reflected it, too!

- *Excellent job redefining our vision and effectively creating buy-in via communication efforts with the entire company. Increased stock price is reflection of our continued efforts to boost profitability and Tim's personal commitment to creating vision around how to get there.*
- *Tim has reinvigorated the culture around the client experience – it's always been our focus but it feels fresh again and a top priority. Tim is extremely persuasive and I appreciate his collaborative style.*

It was showing up in other places besides my reviews. It came in the form of being named a Best Places to Work in Indiana for the first time. Our team was very vocal in their survey feedback that they knew with great clarity that our company was on a good course for the future. It's not that we received perfect scores because we didn't. Yet nearly everything dealing with clarity, mission, vision, opportunity and the future was rock solid.

We began adopting new ways to connect and communicate. We started dipping our toe in the water for ways to harness social media to expand our brand and enhance the clarity of our message. Many members of our team jumped on board with this.

I was still looking for more ways to enhance and support the right language and message internally. Beginning in 2013, I started writing a weekly leadership blog. It has been a great experience and created a lot of value for me and the organization. Every week I have a platform for key issues or to reinforce all the essential stuff. By committing to writing, it has also served as a great accountability partner while showing my team that I'm human, too.

Larry handed out a copy of Joe Calloway's book *Be The Best At What Matters Most* at a conference in 2013. That fall I read Joe's book and connected with him via social media. I was struck by how powerful his simple yet highly effective approach could be when you fully bought in. Through our Twitter conversation in August of 2014 he reinforced the lesson I had learned with Larry.

Today I get asked to speak about how CEOs can better engage with their employees, leadership team and clients using social media and blogging. More than anything, it's about consistency and clarity. Our organization has embraced this with over half of our employees using Twitter for business. Some are already becoming noted experts and thought leaders in their

"What is a leader's most important job? Clarity. First and foremost, clarity about culture. Everyone must be crystal clear about who we are, what we value, and how we treat people. Clarity about culture means that those who violate the culture must leave." ~ Joe Calloway

fields – such as education and public entities or risk management for high net worth individuals. When Larry challenged me on this and pressed me to get better, I had no idea where it would lead.

I realize that so many things – even great ideas – fail because those that we need to embrace the ideas haven't been engaged properly. Over-communicating, with great clarity, has been such a home run for us. I just wish it would not have taken so long for me to figure out. In many ways it's the foundation for everything we do as leaders. Yet so many of us – me included – have missed on this over the years. I've made it a priority to nail this in the future.

Chapter Nine – Leadership Lesson

Tania Bengtsson, Principal at Gibson
Tania has been with Gibson since 2004. Her passion for communication and brand management is a rare commodity in the risk management world.

The Competition Between Clarity And Communication

Clarity and communication are in constant struggle to be at the forefront of every initiative. Yet, one without the other is virtually useless. There's no secret which one comes first. However, a singular focus on one or the other only serves to amplify the issues at hand.

Permeating The Vision

Remaining committed to both clarity and communication is pivotal to success. You must know the vision completely and believe in it. Your commitment will drive excitement and inspiration.

Time to over-communicate. Look for new ways to enhance and support the message. Make sure it is properly communicated with new hires, at every level of your organization, and within every team. Make it a guide for new hire criteria, performance reviews, and recognition.

It is hard work. But **once the foundation is laid throughout the company, it becomes easier to implement change**. Belief in the vision makes the hard work more enjoyable for everyone.

Three out of Patrick Lencioni's *Four Obsessions of an Extraordinary Executive* are illustrated within this chapter: create organizational clarity, over-communicate organizational clarity, and reinforce organizational clarity through human systems.

Having experienced the vision changes at Gibson first-hand, the difference it made to our organization was significant, it was like night and day. Engagement increased, changes got easier, and morale improved significantly. It was a tremendous turning point in our culture and for our growth.

Chapter 10 – In Clarity We Trust

Because of the work we've done with the vision, we are able to move even faster with our team. We aren't perfect. In fact I don't think you can be with this. But our team knows that we are playing for the long haul.

Changing business environments require us to be flexible. We do our best to keep everyone in the loop. We are transparent. This drives trust with our employees. They don't worry about being surprised or blind-sided. Additionally by the organization placing such trust in them, they feel respected and appreciated.

> *We are transparent. This drives trust with our employees.*

An example of our ability to adapt and change would be our team selling and compensation model. It's one of the most revolutionary ideas we've had and has been whole-heartedly adopted by our teams. It's led to tremendous growth and created more value for our clients. They now have a multi-person team to rely on. This keeps our advice fresher. We have additional sets of eyes and ears to observe and listen. And there is built-in perpetuation within their Gibson team.

There was a price for this. When we compared our metrics to others in our industry, we were spending more money on compensation than the others. We were okay with this because our results were better. But to continue investing in our team and other resources and support personnel we needed a little help.

Over the years compensation changes in the sales ranks have been a death blow to morale for many in our industry. It's an area in which many of our peers just give up. Others have decided to wage this fight and have created a toxic environment with their sales team from which they never recovered.

Our salespeople understood why we need to make changes in their compensation. By making our plans just a little less lucrative, we would improve our financial position. This would allow for significant reinvestment in key areas for our clients and salespeople such as more loss control and safety engineers, client software solutions and wellness initiatives. Call it what you want, but we would be shifting dollars from salespeople to resource personnel. How did our team respond?

The salespeople led the effort to revamp our plans. They worked with management to create something fair and equitable that would allow for the necessary reinvestment. They were so committed to our mission to support clients and the long term vision of the organization that they overlooked the personal impact and focused instead on the organization. For the first time in our company's history we had changed the compensation plan without a huge battle. It was a great example of how far we had come. I doubt many other sales teams would have demonstrated the same level of leadership.

In another example, one of our veteran teams had brought on a top notch young salesperson. They mentored, trained and prepared him to be a big part of their sales efforts going forward. They had made a sizeable investment of their time. While this was going on, we lost a person on one of our niche teams. The niche team was poised for huge growth. They had some incredible technical and intellectual assets but were in need of business development skills. The unthinkable happened.

Over several open and candid conversations, we all agreed the niche team needed the new sales talent more than the original team. The young salesperson – now trained and with experience – transitioned over to the niche team. There were no fights, no blood, no nastiness and no manipulation. This just gives testimony to our ability to adapt and keep the organization's best interests at heart.

I firmly place the credit for this on our work to create organizational clarity. It doesn't happen unless we all know the vision and mission and believe in it.

Today, as part of our long term vision, we are aggressively opening a new marketplace in Fort Wayne, Indiana. We have built our plan to be fluid and take advantage of what we can when we can. For instance, after the challenges we had in Indianapolis early on, we appreciate how important strong leadership and connections to the market are. We have been pursuing leadership as well as sales and service personnel for our two primary disciplines as part of a local team in Fort Wayne. We are flexible when it comes to talent and hiring the positions that can be filled first.

On the leadership front, we decided to expand our Board of Directors, and for the first time in our company's history, we added an outside director. We did this to take advantage of a great talent who was transitioning between careers. We have benefited tremendously from his relationships and connections. He's been instrumental in our recruiting, too, connecting us to an incredible talent that recently became our first ever marketplace president.

The best part about this board member? He didn't even come from our industry. His leadership skills, business acumen and connections were more important. Again, the ability to adapt and understand that our plan might change a bit but still fits with the bigger, broader goal, has been key.

Going back to the partner letter seven years ago, I don't believe we would be in a position to execute on changes like having outside board members or hiring a standalone marketplace president without a newfound appreciation for change. Larry sometimes refers to this as the 80% rule. Know most of the game plan and fill in the rest as we go. And this is accepted internally because everyone at Gibson is "rowing in the same direction" as our new board member told me. When you've got it about 80%, just go for it.

Chapter Ten – Leadership Lesson

Jerry Scott, Chief Operating Officer at Gibson
Jerry has been with Gibson since 2013 and is responsible for leadership development and operating performance in all divisions of the company. Prior to joining Gibson, he was a client and engaged with the employee benefits practice.

Trust is Key
The most powerful multiplier in business today is trust. Trust makes employees open to new information and ideas for improvement. Trust brings out creativity, collaboration and the kind of engagement that encourages discretionary effort to drive and improve the business on all levels. Trust is not given or inherited but rather earned and earned over time.

Tim and the leaders at Gibson have earned trust first and foremost though consistent transparency about all aspects of what matters most at Gibson. That starts with clarity on the mission, vision and core values of the company. It continues on a daily, monthly and yearly basis with the strategic plan, as well as annual goals and financial metrics. Employees are openly and enthusiastically educated on progress, including stock price for the ESOP, along with long term revenue, staffing and expansion plans. Virtually nothing is hidden other than sensitive HR related information. **This environment creates massive trust in leadership and a sense of shared destiny.**

When something isn't working in the business and a course correction is needed, the issue is faced openly and all relevant stakeholders are involved in the problem solving process. **Transparency is just as important in dealing with challenges as in sharing good news and information.** This transparency builds trust as employees begin to realize that problems are solved together and they don't have to fear being blind-sided.

Leaders must also be trustworthy and model the behavior they encourage. This comes from a thousand interactions where people are treated with courtesy, respect and consideration. This creates an environment where things are discussed rationally and there is no room for temper or arrogance. Tim has built a culture of leadership based on trust and that trust makes the clarity believable and real.

It is a circle of sorts. **Clarity creates trust and trust enables clarity to become like jet fuel for the culture of the business.**

Chapter 11 – Reflection

All those years ago, we may have sensed the change that was coming to our industry but were paralyzed to act. Perhaps because I wasn't a long time insider at Gibson, I was more willing to see it and felt unencumbered in fighting for what I believed in. It hasn't been easy. We had several events that could or perhaps should have been enough to jolt us forward, but it took the culmination of all of them – conversations stemming from the partner letter, the economic downturn, introspection via my 360 reviews and a limited ability to perpetuate our independence – to put enough pressure on our business model that we took action.

There are so many "what ifs" and I have thought about them often. While our organization was growing, adding new talent, and winning awards, our long time local competitors were sold and even sold again.

We eclipsed the 100 employee mark and won another Best Places To Work award. We built on the 8% increase in our company valuation from 2011 by following it up with a 15% increase in 2012 and a 27% bump in 2013.

In 2014 Principal Financial Group named us one of the 10 Best Companies for Employee Financial Security in the United States. We also have a growing positive reputation on three college campuses with strong risk management and insurance programs. In fact we hired eight college graduates in 2014. They were all high caliber, top of the class college graduates! It's added a lot of craziness, but also much energy and enthusiasm.

Even my Advisor, Larry Linne, in his 2013 annual assessment, scored Gibson as the top company in his network. It was a tremendous honor for our team and outside validation of how far we've come.

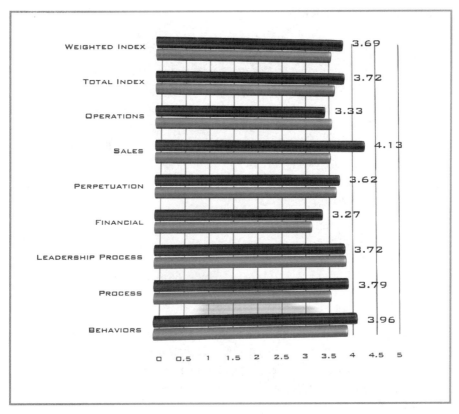

VERTICAL GROWTH INDEX

We've made some poor decisions over the years as well as some good ones. If you would have told me that the most significant driver of whether an idea or strategy would work or not work was organizational clarity, I would have looked at you like you were crazy.

Coming from the national organization, as well as my own belief system, I viewed this cultural stuff as "soft". Sure, I'd do it if and when I had the time. But I believed that our people just needed to be "adults". Show up, do your job, do it well. For that I'd make sure you were paid fairly and treated kindly. Was I ever wrong! Those are important, but not enough.

In late 2012, Greg Downes sent me an email. Attached was the partner letter from 2007. He wrote:

> *I came across this, and I'm sure you probably still have a copy but it was one of your finer moments and set the stage for so much of the change that has taken place over the last 5 ½ years. You had the guts to say what most of the rest of the partner group felt but were too afraid to say. Nice work!*

Getting that email really meant the world to me. To see Greg bringing it up after all these years says a lot about him. He gave me a chance. He allowed for the idea of change to grow and gain steam. He could have easily shut it all down but he didn't.

I think about all the other things that could have prevented our evolution. What if the economy had not turned south and so severely impacted our marketplace? Without it, would we have moved forward with the initiatives we did?

What if we had not placed a renewed emphasis on culture and core values? Would those partners we split with perhaps felt more comfortable staying at Gibson as owners? If so, the pressure of internal perpetuation would not have been as significant and we never would have fully eradicated the poor behavior.

What if my ego and confidence had not been slammed by the 360 reviews? Whether, at the time, I felt they were fair or not, they fueled my deepest motivations to evolve, change and improve.

Yet they all happened and our team ultimately embraced the change we needed. We used the ideas from the partner letter as our guide path. We made improvements. We've gotten better at all of them.

- We are more agile and make decisions much faster now.
- Our value proposition is driving results for our clients.
- We are constantly innovating and improving.
- We are one team, working together for the greater good.
- We know it's all about growth.
- We are collaborative.
- We are candid.
- We have clarity.
- We are built to last.

Today at Gibson we are arguably in a pretty good spot. We are doing quality and impactful work for our clients. This is made possible by our incredible employees.

In fact, one of my senior partners recently said, "We're paving the way for the insurance broker of the future. We haven't reached that next level yet, but we're striving and getting closer all the time. What did we just have? *Another* record year? I say we're just now hitting our stride, Tim. All the hard work is really beginning to pay off!"

We uphold our end of the bargain by providing the basics of a "good job" to our team:

- Interesting and valuable work
- Strong culture
- Good pay
- Committed leadership

The turnaround, while so rewarding, was also more difficult and took longer than I ever imagined. Through every failure I like to think I picked up a few more credit hours toward my degree in leadership.

Ego caused me stumble after stumble. I framed most everything as a courtroom battle in which I would need to prove I was right. This type of personal dominance got me nowhere.

Often I moved so quickly that I didn't take the time to get feedback and input. Instead of avoiding it, I usually stepped in a pile that I created.

Taking the time to survey the landscape would have helped me avoid a number of painful and expensive gaffes.

We forced the implementation of all kinds of tools, strategies, and ideas. I didn't understand that we had not achieved the cultural clarity necessary to effectively leverage them. Most were never adopted, lessening my credibility while wasting precious company resources.

I plugged valuable team members into roles that didn't take advantage of their strengths. This left them unproductive and frustrated while creating major bottlenecks and bad morale with others on the team.

Hubris led us on an ill-planned and poorly executed launch of a new operation in Indianapolis. Only after years of painful financial losses and tough decisions were we able to right the ship in Indy. Opening an office in Indianapolis was the right call, but our timing and planning were off.

We could have used the help of an insider in the local business community, but didn't have one. We came out of the gates as a relative unknown in the marketplace. Having a "friend" would have made for much easier sledding for our team.

We also should have prioritized getting our culture plugged in from the very beginning. We overestimated our ability to provide leadership from afar. These are things we won't miss on again.

Fortunately for me and Gibson, we had two very talented, hardworking and committed team members in Indianapolis who saw all the possibilities of what we could become even on the days when the rest of us only noticed what we were not.

As one of them said to me, "Of course we had challenges and struggles along the way. When you're an entrepreneurial company trying something new, things don't always go as planned." They both hung in there with us from the very beginning and today are partners at Gibson.

During this time I managed to take one of my greatest natural strengths – building personal relationships – and neglect it and those around me.

I was making withdrawals from a number of emotional bank accounts without making any deposits.

As if my personal leadership missteps weren't enough, they fell in the shadow of the Great Recession. The perfect storm had been created by the crashing economy, the exit of several owners, and our bleeding start-up operation in Indianapolis.

By most accounts, this would not have been the optimal time to transition executive leadership for only the 4th time in our then 75 year history. Yet, we made it, preserving our independence.

Looking back now, I can see there were five key leadership traits that made all the difference in my evolution as a leader. What did I have to be?

1. **Resilient:** Without dogged perseverance and a tenacious personal belief system I wouldn't have made it. This doesn't mean that I didn't think about throwing in the towel. Everyone has a breaking point and I almost reached mine. With every story I heard or watched in which other leaders were having success, I felt like a failure. Yet when I found myself getting close to the brink I was able to lean on good friends, colleagues and my spouse to help me through.

   Don't quit at the first sign of trouble but avoid becoming hard headed and stubborn. Just keep working to get it right.

   My take: You have to survive to even have the chance to evolve. The biggest ideas aren't immediately and universally accepted. Don't give up the fight.

2. **Introspective:** For me this didn't happen right away or for the right reasons. Early on, my frustration with the speed and amount of progress led me to question my ideas and approach. But that had a lot more to do with wanting to win for my ego's sake. It took getting crushed in my 360 reviews to truly want to change and change for the right reasons. Even though it's likely that you're

a major contributor to the issues, it's not easy to admit that you might be the problem

There is a fine balance you must find between remaining confident and being willing to question yourself. You have to get honest answers to these questions. My evolution needed – no, required – a combination of mentors, advisors and ultimately the 360 reviews to find my answers.

My take: The ability to self-correct is critical to improving your leadership. Leaders without followers can't drive change. Become self-aware or find others to help you.

3. **Adaptive:** Will you keep organizational success as your guiding light or will you allow tradition and legacy to burden your ambitions? Learning to live with and actually embrace change will help you carry the day. Nothing is static these days and you can't afford to be either. Transform or die. It's a message you have to be communicating to your team all the time. The more prepared they are to live in a fluid and evolving world, the easier it will be to implement necessary change in your organization.

   You can still provide constants to them via your core values. As an example, one of our values is *Integrity Matters: Always do the right thing.* Our team knows that no matter what changes in the business world, we will always do business the right way. You see, the heart of our culture is not up for debate. Our team knows they can take that to the bank!

   My take: Be ready, willing and able to take advantage of opportunities even if they collide with history and tradition. Even Sun Tzu said leaders that can modify tactics are "heaven sent".

4. **Collaborative:** "Command and control" leadership won't fly with today's multi-generational and diverse workforce. Collaboration is about input and influence versus coercion. Your people want to be heard, understood and most importantly, actively involved. Besides, you don't have the market for good ideas cornered. Bring

them into the loop and treat them like owners. Be transparent, fair and accountable to them as you would a partner. You will be rewarded handsomely.

Additionally when you can harness the creative power and intellectual energy of a team, you will see exponential growth in your ability to innovate. Give your people a chance to contribute and they'll likely surprise you.

My take: Buy-in will occur more quickly and deeply when your team has been a part of the process. Your best ideas can become even better when challenged and critiqued by others.

5. **Clear:** You need to have everyone marching to the same beat. This requires great organizational clarity. Start with a compelling mission, create your grand vision and live your core values. Help everyone understand what's in it for them and how they can contribute. Your language and actions will drive this. It's the not-so-secret sauce.

No strategy or tactic can trump organizational clarity. Everything else becomes easier when it's right. Embracing change, faster decision making, collaboration, team work… they all become the norm when you have clarity.

My take: Clarity creates an organizational road map to success. It drives faster and better decision making while increasing trust.

Make no mistake; it took a lot to get here. We constantly kept working, tinkering, and changing to get better.

There has been a price to our success. We've had the pedal down to the floorboard for many years now. I sense we are dealing with some organizational fatigue. Can we stop and take a break? Most organizations don't make it this far up the mountain. Isn't this good enough?

The only problem with that is, as one of my clients fondly says, "Once you set your pack

> *"Once you set your pack down, it's way too tempting to stay and enjoy the view."*

down, it's way too tempting to stay and enjoy the view." I worry about this a lot. How can I keep our team focused and forging ahead? Complacency has to be avoided at all costs. It's what got us in trouble in the first place.

What inspires me is to know the tremendous potential we have to be great. It is nice to have made it this far up the mountain, but we're on a mission to the top! A question I have to ask myself is if I have what it takes? Do I have the fierce resolve necessary to take us to the next level? Gibson will need me to lead in new ways. I know this will require me to grow and evolve again.

Anyone who thinks leaders are simply born, or alternatively can be just be created with a degree or diploma, will find they are both dead wrong. The terrain is constantly changing. You have to evolve and grow with it. And sometimes it even requires a revolutionary shift.

> *The terrain is constantly changing. You have to evolve and grow with it.*

We worked so hard to achieve clarity and I realize that it's not a one-time thing. It's not a project. It has to be a part of everything we do. I need to freshen up my message and take it back out to our people again. After all, our workforce is now one third millennial! I need to make sure my communication and language is working for them and our veterans.

As we grow and expand into new markets, I am less able to be personally in front of all of our employees. I've begun to take advantage of video conferencing and Brainshark presentations to keep my message personal while still communicating regularly. We also created a new all company email subject line – "In The Loop" – for important organizational messages from me.

I have to be confident that I'm using the right language at all times. Something that comes from me takes on a different level of seriousness and importance. I enjoy using humor in my interactions but I have to be a little more careful so that I don't convey something unintended.

I am working hard at connecting with other leaders and peer groups that can help me grow. I joined Young Presidents' Organization (YPO) to gain a broader perspective and a source of ideas and knowledge. We plan to make some acquisitions in the coming year. I've had no experience with this but was able to sit down with a member of my YPO Forum who deals in M&As. I have seen the value of surrounding myself with people smarter and more experienced than I am.

This was also a driving factor in appointing our first ever outside board member. I know I need to be pushed and challenged. I can't become satisfied. Like everyone else, I only know what I know. Outside perspective can change that dynamic. But it also gave me a new level of accountability with our board.

I need my advisors, like Larry, to help me as well. Answering to someone completely outside your organization can be powerful when done right.

In the community, I'm now clearly seen as the leader of Gibson, versus Greg or Dave. While I never had a poor personal brand, I know that I'm under a microscope now. My personal brand is a significant part of the Gibson brand. I'm careful to keep that in mind in all my interactions. I owe that to Gibson and my fellow employees. It's the reality of my role.

I don't have all the answers. Heck, I don't even know all the questions to ask. And I believe it's a lot more important to have the right questions versus the right answers. Both are needed, but the questions start the process. This is where leaders need to ensure they have outside support. I know I need people around me that ask or inspire the tough questions. They are necessary for any evolutionary or revolutionary change in leadership.

With our growth, I'm less and less able to personally impact our results. I have to influence them. This means relying on the other members of my executive leadership team, our Board and our managers.

"Being fiercely independent makes us so dependent on each other," said one of my partners. In other companies it's all about 'me'. It's about 'we' at Gibson." He's right. And that's a big part of what drives us all to keep getting better. We don't want to let our teammates down!

With that in mind, I know I have to get better at setting expectations and holding my team accountable. I have to resist the urge to insert myself in things I don't need to be in. I have to give up more control. It's been a struggle, but I'm working on it.

I was fortunate to be born with some God-given talents and had good parenting growing up. From coaches in school, to professors in college, to the many mentors during my career, I've always had leaders to emulate and learn from. This type of learning gets trickier but more important the higher you climb.

The point is I can't ask my people and my organization to embrace change if I can't do the same. Whatever skills got me here will likely remain helpful but they won't be enough.

> *I can't ask my people and my organization to embrace change if I can't do the same.*

While some of the challenges leaders face can be overwhelming, they also keep us humble and searching. Personal evolution can be painful, but there is something deeply moving to me in knowing that I have so much room for improvement and growth. Besides, it's not like I have a choice. The rapidly shifting environment of today's business world will require it. Evolve or die.

When I lived in Arizona I used to hike Camelback Mountain quite a bit. It overlooks The Phoenician resort in Scottsdale. On the mountain, the guests of the resort were always a dead giveaway. They were typically dressed in street clothes and not carrying any water. Without fail, they would declare victory as they approached "the summit" only to realize they had only come to the top of the camel's back and still had the toughest and final third of the hike to go.

That's where we are at. We've come a long way and accomplished much, but we aren't there yet. Things are only going to get more challenging. Are we ready for the speed and complexity of the emerging risks businesses are facing? We're about to find out!

Chapter Eleven – Leadership Lesson

Andrew Graman, Client Manager at Gibson
Andrew joined Gibson in 2013 and works in the employee benefits practice.

It Was Contagious
A month into my senior year at Indiana State University, I received an email from the CEO of a regional brokerage firm asking to meet. I had only heard about his company once or twice, and I had plenty of offers on the table, including one in Arizona resulting from an extraordinary internship. *Who is Gibson and what's in South Bend besides Notre Dame?* Feeling a little full of myself, I thought *Good Luck, Mr. Leman* as he walked through the door of a popular spot on campus.

In a few short hours, my perception of the post-grad job search was turned upside down. I immediately noticed that Tim kept bringing everything back to culture and "vision" for the future of Gibson. This focus was unlike anything I had ever experienced in my gauntlet of interviews, conversations with human resource managers, and job offers. He wasn't selling an entry-level job; **he was selling a career path and a part in the vision for Gibson**!

The Next Generation
Up to 50% of the insurance industry's workforce will be retiring over the next 5 to 10 years. In order to maintain our independence, recruiting the next generation is a necessity! Our workforce at Gibson is one third millennial, with this percentage only likely increasing in the coming years. Generational diversity brings challenges and opportunities that require adaptation and collaboration. The alternative - missing out on the unique talents and tendencies of Boomers, Gen X, and the millennials - can diminish the progress of any organization.

A big challenge for our recent college graduates, including myself, is we have only seen what a good job looks like. With this utopic view could come the tendency of complacency from those who did not experience the struggles noted in the early chapters of this book. **We must stay innovative and adapt to the ever-changing environment we live in to avoid repeating our past.**

Culture Isn't "Soft"

We have progressed into an employer of choice in the marketplace. How do I know? College students now come to the recent college graduates at Gibson asking if there are internships and full-time positions available. This is a defining difference from years past when Gibson was a small blip on the radar.

People ask how the culture at Gibson is different compared to other companies, and the best way to describe the difference is through a visual representation. Imagine hiking up a large mountain on a trail full of twists and turns. Fog covers the top of the mountain so no one can see the final destination: our common goal. Our guides are our executive leadership, with everyone helping each other along the way. People volunteer to fill the gaps left by those who are no longer on the hike, and new people join, adding their unique talents and perspectives. The trail isn't always clear of obstacles, and the weather isn't always fair; however, the combination of **trust in leadership and focus on the common goal keeps us always pushing upward**.

What's Next? – *By Larry Linne, CEO InCite Performance Group*

I know Tim spends his "thinking time" wondering if he has done enough? He and Gibson have experienced a great deal of success over the past several years. They've built a great team and are positioned for the long haul. As long as they stay true to their vision, mission and values, while striving to constantly improve, will they get where they want to go? My gut tells me it won't be enough.

Emerging business risks require a fresh look and new solutions. There will be an abundance of challenges and opportunities for leaders in all industries. The speed of business seems to be increasing at an almost exponential pace. An aging workforce, generational differences, productivity, the technology revolution, disaster preparedness, organizational communication, reputational risk and emerging human resource challenges are all significant. And they are evolving by the day.

The companies that can win at these issues will win the whole game. As Lencioni writes, healthy businesses operate with "minimal politics and confusion" as well as "high degrees of morale and productivity, and very low turnover."

To that end, Tim and I have agreed to focus our monthly coaching over the next year on emerging issues. I know this process will be instrumental in helping him and Gibson meet the challenge of these dynamic issues.

We will document Gibson's learning, successes, failures, and outcomes in taking on these emerging issues, as well as Tim's progress as a leader. Here is a sneak preview.

Workforce

- **Connecting with young professionals**

  With America's workforce aging rapidly we will find ourselves with a huge talent gap in the very near future. We need to bring in young professionals and help them develop into contributing team members as quickly as possible. The need is there. But how do we find, and more importantly retain, the top young talent?

  Gibson's workforce is now one third millennial! They can't afford to see their investment walk away after a few years. This is high risk and high reward. What do they need to do to win the war for young talent?

  This is a complex issue. They have to ensure their hiring practices, onboarding strategies and company culture are receptive to millennials and provide long term growth opportunities. Early research suggests young professionals will have multiple jobs in their careers. They believe they can (and must) change that trend with the right strategies and tactics.

  What does this emerging generation look like?

  According to a Forbes.com's May 2013 "Surprising facts about millennials in the workplace" article:

    o 6 in 10 millennials are not considering a career in business.
    o 59% of business decision makers and 62% of higher education influential types give recent college graduates a C grade or lower for preparedness in their first jobs.
    o 68% of corporate recruiters say it is difficult for their organizations to manage millennials.

o   74% of non-millennials agree that millennials offer different skills and work styles which add value to the workplace.

o   74% agree that businesses must partner with colleges and universities to provide business curriculums that properly prepare students for the workplace.

Millennials are necessary and valuable to the future of our businesses. But they are different. They are educated differently, motivated differently, and have a different sense of purpose. Businesses will need to understand the cultural make up of this generation yet also treat them as individuals, unique, and... different.

Without effective leadership of this generation, they will not be able to survive the future.

- **Creating balance for and with boomers**

Boomers were the first generation to define the generations. How they transition out of the workforce over the next fifteen years will be one of the most impactful and influencing changes businesses have ever seen.

My research on the boomer generation has revealed the following:

1. The majority of boomers define their personal value by what they do for a living and what they own. Many view leaving their job as a loss of personal value and they thwart the possibility of departing the workplace. Plain and simple, they are struggling to leave their jobs.

2. Our business economy has historically experienced generation after generation transition out of their primary work between the ages of 62 and 65. Only a few outliers remain in the workforce after age 68. Boomers are already staying at work longer and many people are predicting the majority will work well into their 70s.

The expenses associated with the perpetuation phenomena of this generation could be the largest cost businesses face in the next 20 years. They will impact companies in a number of different ways including: health care, absenteeism, presenteeism, maximizing productivity, let alone a lack of interest in innovation and using new technologies.

Gibson has an incredible veteran workforce. Their boomers are loaded with years of technical and on-the-job training and knowledge. They have many of them paired with young professionals, transitioning their intellectual capital to the next generation. But what is next?

This is a huge challenge in that a boomer's work often defines them. This becomes a problem when boomers think of retirement. If they leave work, they may lose their personal perceived value. For others, they continue to have much to add but are interested in easing into a reduced schedule. How can businesses leverage this tremendous asset as boomers transition into the next phase of their lives?

It should also be an objective to treat this generation with dignity and respect. The best companies want to remain focused on the human side of things. It takes extra thought and planning to allow boomers to exit the business gracefully and with the respect they deserve.

- **HR needs to rewrite the rules**

As of December 2014, the "Netflix Culture: Freedom and Responsibility" presentation on Slideshare.net had 10,236,319 hits. If you are one of the few who have not seen it, the presentation describes the culture at Netflix. It is a powerful message of how to lead people. Businesses are going to be competing for the best talent in the market. To do so, they must have the best culture. HR procedures, systems, and structure will be critical to create this perfect culture.

I recently met with an insurance agency principal who was part of a bank environment. He said the bank went to a new hourly computerized check in system for employees. The bank decided all employees needed to use this system. So, high level professional insurance consultants were now required to check in and check out when they left their desks. If they were late for work or after lunch, they were required to submit a note to their supervisor as to the reason why. If you are cringing while reading this, you will understand what I mean when I say HR will have an influence on our success in the future.

When you compare a Netflix model of NO monitoring of time off to a bank who monitors desk time by the minute, who do you believe will win the future workforce? Also, who will win the top talent?

The best companies won't be traditional in their approach to human resources. All organizations have to become more creative. That might mean building out flexible work initiatives, such as the summer hours program Gibson implemented in 2014. I recently implemented unlimited PTO at my company. The attractive companies will utilize HR policies that address employees working from home, job sharing, personal development, working on teams, and more.

It also means adapting to the diverse needs of a workforce. HR practices need to position a company as the employer of choice. The war for talent won't be won without thoughtful and innovative action in this area.

HR will no longer be simply a department or a title in a company. We are moving quickly toward an era that will require us to measure the true return on human capital.

Development

- ### Embrace the need for a culture of learning

    Are you aware of the terms petabyte or exabyte? These are the next generation of terms that will be used to measure data. The petabyte is 1000x larger than the terabyte. The exabyte is 1000x larger than the petabyte. The fact that these titles exist makes it clear that information is coming to us faster than any time in history. So fast that it is hard to keep up!

    What does this information mean to a growing organization? When data and information is available, those who can extract from it, learn from it, and become a fast moving and nimble organization will be able to compete and win in the future.

    It is important to remain intellectually curious. The minute you think you've got it all figured out is the exact point you stop being valuable to your clients, your people and your community. Organizations that take advantage of big data, continuous learning, and a focus on intellectual growth will lead their industries.

    The advisors at InCite continue to press our member organizations: "We have to be prepared that more than ½ of what we do and how we do it for our clients in the next 5-7 years may not even be invented yet."

    I first shared this message back in 2009 to the insurance industry. And it has proven quite true. Today we have new communication models and new resources available to us that are new since 2009.

    I've always enjoyed learning. And I try to find new ways to acquire and absorb information. Twitter, LinkedIn, podcasts and apps on my smartphone are all new sources of fresh content. The trick is to learn how to narrow the flow of information down to the highest value and impact. And then do something with it.

As you heard in Tim's story, Gibson had always valued continuing education in their organization. They continue to evolve in this area in order to stay on top of cutting edge ideas and solutions. No longer will just the standard industry trade magazines suffice. As business models evolve to cover a broad enterprise level of client risk, so too must our learning.

Additionally, companies that build intellectual property will have an advantage in the market. A learning culture will thrive on innovation, creativity, and building new intellectual property for our clients. This cultural shift and development will have the added benefit of being attractive to young professionals while giving your clients a world class product.

- **Bring increased value to the company by growing personal brands**

  Proactive brand management can amplify your expertise in the marketplace. Many of the members in my network are engaged in regular delivery of content to employers. They have seen an increase in their stature and reputation. They are seen as subject matter experts and problem solvers. The spend very little time on old school business development methods like cold calling, and instead invest that time in growing their knowledge. Yet, in spite of proven success and growth, many traditional insurance brokers have not embraced this approach.

  In 2014 I wrote a book with Patrick Sitkins called *Brand Aid – Taking Control of Your Reputation before Everyone Else Does.* This book has had great success across North America. The concept of managing your reputation is a cultural imperative in today's world of highly accessible information. Your people can damage or build a powerful personal brand in a very short amount of time. Organizations will need to manage these brands and coordinate the efforts to align with the company brand.

  My team researched over 10,000 business decision makers and learned that 84% of these individuals will look up a salesperson online before meeting with them. Buyers are now doing more research before buying than ever. That, along with social media and internet footprints, creates a need for everyone to manage their brand.

It doesn't take very long to name individuals who have taken down companies or big brands. Yes, ONE PERSON can damage the brand of a company. The worst example in the past few years has been Jerry Sandusky. He single-handedly brought down Penn State University. It will take years for this prestigious institution to fully recover from one assistant coach's brand damage.

- **Build your communication strategy**

If companies like Toyota can have global collaboration on their design teams to speed up new car production by a few years, the rest of us can certainly enhance our communication techniques. Tools such as Yammer, Chatter and Evernote Work Chat are helping organizations have more real time communications to foster collaborative environments. Linear communication tools are going to rapidly decline. Social media, collaborative communication tools, and maybe even things that have yet to be invented, will become essential parts of healthy organizations.

If you're growing you will need to be even more purposeful than ever with language, as it plays such a key role in driving culture. You will need to employ a strategy to cascade the messaging beyond yourself and the executive team.

You will also need to consider collaborative communication tools as part of your communication strategies since email is not the most productive means of communication in a firm with some complexity.

These items will become very critical to Gibson as they grow, open new offices, and acquire other organizations.

- **It's time for a new performance management system**

Amazon.com has 20,702 books available on performance management. When I'm asked to speak, more than 50% of the requests are about performance management. Why is performance management such a hot topic?

I believe the primary reason is because the workforce keeps evolving and old systems aren't working. There is also a desire to have a very high return on human capital. The combination of a poor system and rapid change will require us to determine new methods of maximizing performance.

The best companies will need to address intrinsic motivation and reverse performance management strategies (employees owning the behaviors and communicating to management how they are doing), and why these strategies are so powerful in giving "purpose in work".

Employers need to ensure they're meeting the needs of their employees to receive regular feedback and updates on how they are doing. Top employers will help them establish a plan for their future.

A key point I have observed is that if an individual doesn't know something, they tend to create their own reality. That's why clarity is one of the most important things you can give to those you lead. By providing clarity on what really matters, they will be able commit effort to the job and not to wondering about themselves.

Risk Management

- **Utilizing the right technology solutions**

Recently I was looking at a Cyber Insurance Risk PowerPoint training document from 2001. I couldn't believe how much has changed in the past 14 years. It was comical to read about the predictions of how many businesses will have computers and how many people will use the internet. I remember when the thought of being on cloud based systems versus having our own hardware for all our data was unaffordable, if even a little unthinkable, just five years ago.

Automation, efficiency and the ability to harness information will be key to our growth. I bet by 2020 more than half of the touches and methods we use today will be replaced by something that doesn't even exist right now. Promising, but untested, solutions will come at us quickly and companies need to make smart decisions about each one of them.

Chasing IT will be the norm for many organizations. The most productive companies will monitor technological innovations, forecast change, and strive to build processes and systems in order to be a leader in technology.

The final concern with technology is cyber protection. Security is constantly being tested and challenged by technology. Protection of data and critical client information must be a continued priority.

- **Withstanding a major disaster, breach or reputational hit**

    Every CEO must understand their role as a risk manager. Risk identification is critical.

    Every other year Lloyds of London conducts a risk survey of global CEOs to learn about their awareness and concerns regarding risks. In 2014, KPMG also did a study on CEOs and discovered that many claimed they fell short in the area of risk management. Both of these reports clearly identify the changing and emerging environment of risks and how prepared CEOs are for these changes.

    As a CEO of a company that is responsible for helping our clients manage risk, I have an even greater concern about issues in these reports:

ote.

1. New and emerging risks are pushing to the top of the "concerns" and "lack of prepared" lists. Risks like cyber, reputation, social media, global warfare, and hiring/retaining employees, are areas of big concern (as they should be), but CEOs are not adequately prepared for the changes.

2. The speed of new technology is outpacing insurance products and security systems. 85% of data breaches are due to human error such as when someone opens an email, leaves a computer on at night connected to Wi-Fi, or enters sites that extract information.

   So, if technology is moving faster than we can protect through security measures and insurance, businesses are going to need to invest more in prevention and mitigation strategies. This means more training of employees, teaching new behaviors to employees, and preparing for fast reputation management if and when something goes wrong. Ignoring the possibility of a breach is not a reasonable strategy. Simply insuring the loss is also not an acceptable risk management strategy. Employers will need to put a full court press on prevention, mitigation, financing, and transferring risk when it comes to technology.

3. Alternative risk financing (compared to traditional insurance products) is a growing field. Captive insurance arrangements, exchanges for health benefits, risk retention, and self-insurance are all gaining steam. These represent tools that could be part of a broader solution, but they also require a deeper commitment from company leadership.

4. According to the Lloyds Risk Index survey in 2011 and 2013, reputational risks are impacting at least 80% of the top 1000 companies in the world. Reputation management is critical in the new world of social media and gotcha journalism.

- **The CEO's role in company-wide risk management**

The direction of an organization will ultimately be driven from risk identification and management. Great CEOs will have a tremendous amount of information and data to be able to identify risk opportunities and risks to avoid.

Effective risk management can be structured into a very organized manner:

1. As a leader you and your team need to **identify** and **organize** the risks your organization faces. You should think of them as Strategic, Business or Hazard risks. Some of the hazard risks, such as a building burning down, will be easier to think about. Business and strategic risks that involve workforce, perpetuation or reputational issues can be more difficult. Categorizing them allows for combining issues and creating a clearer picture.

2. You must **quantify** your risks. This helps you **prioritize** how you will address them. Experience says that if you put significant effort into this process you'll likely come away a bit overwhelmed. That's okay and probably means you've given this it's proper due. The quantification process often leads to a change in company thinking.

3. Create a formal **plan** and systematically **implement** it. Your risk management plan will serve as a guide for the overall organization and ensure the ongoing engagement with the action items.

When CEOs develop clarity of risk and lead an organization strategically through these risks, the organization will thrive. This is only amplified for an organization like Gibson given the business its in. They have to nail it for themselves and their clients.

These are the items in our sights today. With the speed of information, and change that is taking place in the world today, we will certainly add to the list.

As Tim and I work through these emerging risks at Gibson, we intend to document our collective experience – the good, the bad and the ugly – in an effort to help others. Stay tuned!

Acknowledgements

To my amazing wife Kimra, without your steadfast support there wouldn't be a story

Jack, Will and Gracie, thanks for giving up some "Dad time" so I could take a shot at this book

To my informal but incredibly gracious editorial committee, your ideas, edits and critique were invaluable: Katie, Tania, Brandon, Charlie, Ray, Brock, Tommy & Mom

Thank you Scott Franko for bringing the design to life

To Dr. Coleman, Steve Pahl and Tony Hutti: thank you for inspiring the best from me over the years

Many thanks to my Willis colleagues for giving a young guy long on potential, but short on experience, the opportunity of a lifetime and showing him what excellence looks like

I'm thankful for our clients, the reason we are in business

To all of my fellow employee owners at Gibson, one word: #GESOP

Dave, Greg and my Gibson partners past and present: your legacy of being committed for the long haul lives on

To my friend Larry Linne, thanks for your partnership and for pushing me to put this story into words